Four Score and More

10 Suggestions for My Grandchildren

Randall L. Braddom MD, FAAPMR, FABEM

Newhouse Creative Group

ImPress Publishing Services

This book is dedicated to my grandchildren, who range in age from four to 25.

A big thank you to my children and their spouses for having such wonderful children.

Another thank you to my friend and co-worker Maria Salerno for her editing skills.

Contents

Preface   VII

1. Suggestion #1: Get Some Exercise and   1
    Stay Fit

2. Suggestion #2: Never Stop Learning   23

3. Suggestion #3. Be Willing to Risk Fail-   32
    ure

4. Suggestion #4: Be a Good Listener   39

5. Suggestion #5: Keep Your Spousal Re-   47
    lationship Fresh

6. Suggestion #6: Plan and Save for Retire-   59
    ment

7. Suggestion #7: Be Trusting, but Don't   84
    be Gullible

8. Suggestion #8: Celebrate that America   105
    is Multiethnic, Multicultural, and Mul-
    tireligious

9. Suggestion #9: Don't Join Organiza-   122
    tions that Discriminate

10. Suggestion #10: View Change as an Op-   148
    portunity

Preface

On the occasion of my 80th birthday, my children and grandchildren threw a wonderful party for me. Since I am a natural extrovert, I was allotted one hour to "do my act" for them. So I told a few of my favorite jokes, had a joke quiz for them, read a story I had composed that consisted entirely of metaphors, and gave them some suggestions for living. They don't really need these suggestions as they are all doing extremely well, are very intelligent, well educated, and are outstanding people in every way. My children will attest that when they were growing up I typically had strong opinions of what they were and were not allowed to do. However, once they reached 18 years of age, I felt that it was their turn to run their lives. Unless they asked me a direct question, I didn't give them any advice, except by example. I have tried to live my life in such a way that it would be a good example for them...rather than preaching to them. Of course, I haven't always been the best example for them, but I have tried.

I always felt that as adults, my children and grandchildren had the right and the need to explore and make mistakes. Hopefully any mistakes they make will not be cataclysmic...just painful enough to learn from. But I still have opinions, just like I did when they were growing up...but many of them have changed after my 80 years of existence. So I decided to write down some of them in this booklet. I don't know if my children or grandchildren will actually read them, but I hope so. I would also ask them to keep this booklet and dust it off in about 30-40 years and see if the suggestions are still relevant.

The style of this booklet is an "op-ed." I didn't heavily annotate the booklet like an academic paper. Even if you are not one of my direct descendants, you are welcome to read this booklet and draw your own conclusions. Hopefully the booklet will be food for thought, and maybe you will even be inspired to write a similar booklet for your own children and grandchildren.

I must admit that I have a number of additional opinions that I did not include in the booklet because I did not feel qualified to write about them. For example, I believe that global warming is an existential threat to our planet and to all humans. However, I left it out of the booklet because I am not a climatologist and I don't have any credentials that would qualify me to write such a chapter.

Enjoy!

Randall L. Braddom MD

Suggestion #1: Get Some Exercise and Stay Fit

D on't get your exercise by jumping to conclusions!

Most Americans no longer have to exercise to
get through their daily lives. Exercise is no longer
an automatic part of our daily life or work. Just a
few generations ago Americans had to do physical
labor to survive. Their jobs required manual labor, and even their homes typically required physical tasks like shoveling coal or cutting wood. Now
in our society many people go to work in a car,
take a short walk from the car to the elevator of
their office building, sit in a cubicle with a phone
and a computer, and then reverse the process to
get home. I think this lack of exercise has probably

gotten even worse with the post-Covid pandemic move to working at home. In our homes we have appliances that take most of the work out of household chores, from laundry to washing dishes. It would seem that this lack of having to do exercise because of the changes in our lifestyles would be a good thing...and in many ways it is. The main problem with it, however, is that since exercise is no longer an automatic part of our lifestyle, we now must CHOOSE TO EXERCISE.

I think most would agree that as a nation we have become more obese over the course of the last few generations. The Centers for Disease Control (CDC) reports that our obesity rate continues to rise. It has gone from 30.5% of the adult population in 1999-2000 to 41.9% in 2017-2020. Obesity varies widely by state. In 2018 the highest rate of obesity was in Mississippi at 39.5%, with the lowest at 23.0% in Colorado.

This increasing obesity is odd because our genetics haven't really changed much in the last few decades. I personally believe that science will ultimately prove that that most obesity (probably at least 60% of it) is genetic. But there hasn't been a recent change in our genetics that would explain our increasing national rate of obesity. One of the major factors producing this increasing obesity is the ready availability of high fat and high calorie foods and snacks. As a nation we have become addicted to foods that are high in fat, sugar, and also in salt....in foods that are highly processed. Since those kinds of foods are what we like and what will sell, our food companies just keep turning out more of them. Evolution takes thousands of years to make us more adaptive to our environment...not just a few generations. Our genetics in regard to food intake probably evolved long ago during the caveman and hunter-gatherer periods of human history. I think it is likely that our current genome has no good answer to a diet of high sugar, fat and salt.

But I think that despite this avalanche of high sugar, high fat and high salt foods, perhaps the main cause for obesity increasing in the USA is our lack of adequate exercise. I mentioned above that most Americans now don't have a job that requires a lot of exercise, and now must CHOOSE TO EXERCISE. There are exceptions, of course, such as the job of the classic mail carrier...in which the carrier walks miles a day in all types of weather delivering the mail door to door on foot. In the past, the medical community didn't get too worried about people not getting exercise...they had to exercise to survive. Now that we have to CHOOSE TO EXERCISE, are Americans actually and intentionally building exercise into their lifestyle and CHOOSING to EXERCISE? The answer is mixed, but overall Americans are not getting the exercise they need to keep their bodies healthy.

Why do you need to exercise? It seems that a life of leisure would be a good thing. If you were God and you were designing humans through an evolutionary process...why would you require that humans exercise to maintain their strength and health? I lecture from time to time around the country on the benefits of exercise, and I have given this issue some serious thought. What I have come up with so far is that we are made to be pluripotential. That is, our bodies are designed to allow us to change them to accomplish what we need or want to do. There are many kinds of "aerobic" exercise, including running, walking, tennis, racquetball, pickleball, etc. I will focus on one popular type of aerobic exercise, running. You can use this same kind of analysis for any other exercise you choose. If you want to be a runner you can start out by running a short distance per day and then gradually building up your mileage until you are running multiple miles per week. Your body will slowly adapt to do this, including improvements in the cardiac and pulmonary systems...and increases in cardiac output, as well as reductions in heart rate and blood pressure. Provided that you don't try to become a marathon runner overnight...your body will gradually adapt so that most people can run long distances without injury. (Caveat: If you are over 40 or have any personal cardiac history or family cardiac history, see your physician before starting any vigorous exercise program). This practice of starting out slowly and gradually increasing your mileage is also true for a walking program or any aerobic exercise.

Here are some specific statements about running as an exercise (which also apply to a walking program):

1. It has the advantage that you don't have to have any friends to do it. You don't have to spend time getting together a group of people (such as 18 for baseball or 2-4 for pickleball), since you can run by yourself

if necessary. In my experience it is always more fun to exercise in a group, but running doesn't require that. All you really need is a good pair of running shoes. It also fits into your schedule...you can run any time you have the time. Runners tend to get "addicted" to running and they begin to plan their day around their run, rather than planning their run around their day.

2. Running can be done almost anywhere, and in almost all kinds of weather. Be careful on hot days that you don't become overheated, and be careful on cold days that you don't develop hypothermia or frostbite.

3. Your body needs time to adapt, so don't increase your mileage more than 10% per week.

4. It is safer to run in a group. Call me old fashioned, but I think anyone, especially women and children, should not put themselves in danger by running alone through isolated or dark areas.

5. Some runners become ultramarathoners, and can run 100 or more miles per day. Humans appear to be able to outrun any other land animal. We can't outrun a horse, for example, at a one mile distance; but we can outrun a horse over long distances. Fortunately, to get most of the health benefits of long distance running you don't have to run really long distances like marathons or ultramarathons. If you can run shorter distances such as 5K or 10K runs, you are probably getting most of the health benefits that distance running offers (more on this below).

6. Running will cause you to lose weight,

which will allow you to run even longer distances. As a rule of thumb the lighter you are the faster you can run long distances. For example, if you want to be really competitive as a marathon runner, you probably can't weigh more than two pounds per inch of body height.

7. Long distance running requires that you have endurance. The evolutionary process for endurance was not very democratic and did not leave all of us with the same level of inherent capacity for endurance. Endurance has many physiologic requirements, but the basic one is the ability to burn oxygen as quickly and efficiently as possible. Oxygen is burned in the cells of our body mainly through a chemical process in the mitochondria. We can measure this in a laboratory with what is referred to as the VO_2 max. This is how many milliliters of oxygen we can

burn per kilogram of body weight per minute. Most of us are born with the ability to burn about 30-50 milliliters of oxygen per kilogram per minute. Some people, however, are born with values as high as 80, which can be increased with aerobic training such as long distance running or cross country skiing. A very high VO_2 is a genetic gift, and those who have this gift typically win the local, national, and international marathon races. This process of burning oxygen occurs mainly in the mitochondria, which are contained in our cells, especially muscle cells. (By the way, mitochondrial DNA is inherited only from your mother...so if you want to be a great runner you should try to be the child of a woman with an outstanding VO_2).

Let's say however, that what you want to become is not a runner but a weightlifter or body builder. You would start out lifting light weights and slowly building up the amount of weight you lift. Your body will respond in many ways, but especially by enlarging (or as we say "hypertrophying") your muscles. You will start to look like a weightlifter and become substantially stronger. (Warning: The use of heavy free weights can be very dangerous. If you want to use free weights like barbells, you need to get some training at your local health club or YMCA. Also, do not lift heavy free weights alone...it is just like swimming...always have a buddy (spotter) with you).

So my point is that your body can be trained to be able to do much of what you want it to do or need it to do. I think the price that you pay for this "pluripotentiality" is that if you do nothing, your body slowly becomes nothing.

In general the more exercise you do the better it is for you. The 2018 "Physical Activity Guidelines" for Americans that was published in the medical journal *JAMA* recommended a minimum of 150-300 minutes/week of moderate physical activity, or 75-150 minutes/week of vigorous physical activity (or a combination of both). Moderate activities included walking, lower-intensity exercise, weightlifting, and calisthenics. Vigorous activities included running, swimming, bicycling, squash, racketball, tennis, working outdoors, and climbing stairs.

In a massive study recently published in the medical journal *Circulation*, multiple questionnaires were sent to and received from 116,000 people over a period of 30 years. The study looked at the question of how much exercise was needed to lower a person's risk of mortality (what doctors call the all-cause mortality rate). The study analyzed the exercise level and other health aspects of these subjects and compared that to their mortality rate. The results showed that those meeting either the moderate exercise guideline or the vigorous exercise guideline lowered their all-cause mortality and their cardiovascular disease mortality rate by 60% to 70%. This study also looked at the issue of doing more exercise than suggested by the "activity guidelines for Americans," to see if the mortality rate could be lowered even more. For those who doubled the time spent in moderate exercise, the death rate went down an additional 3-14%.

One of the things that discourages some people from exercising is that they feel they don't have the time or interest in spending a significant amount of time exercising, especially enough time to meet the "physical activity guidelines" noted above. Exercising for the time required by the "Activity Guidelines for Americans" can be done without even working up much of a sweat. For example, you could take a one hour walk at lunchtime Monday through Friday and that would be 300 minutes of moderate exercise per week...instead of having a heavy lunch that could leave you sluggish for the rest of the afternoon. The good news for "couch potatoes" is that science is now showing that even a small amount of exercise helps...just doing a single flight of stairs has a positive impact...the exercise benefit doesn't just happen with a long and time-consuming program lasting hours per week. Every little bit helps!

Here are some tips I have found helpful on how to encourage yourself to CHOOSE to exercise:

1. <u>Regard the time you exercise as "time spent for yourself"</u> and enthusiastically agree with the supposition that you "earned and deserve this time."

2. <u>Be realistic about the amount of time you can spend on exercise</u>...which depends on your life circumstances. For example, I am personally not a golfer...because the chunk of time it takes to play golf just doesn't fit with my work schedule and lifestyle. But for others, a couple rounds of golf each week might fit very well into their lifestyle.

3. <u>Be realistic about the expense of the exercise</u>...can you afford it? For example, running or walking just requires a good pair of shoes, as opposed to hundreds of dollars per year to play indoor racquetball or to go skiing.

4. <u>Use one of your personality characteristics to encourage you exercise</u>. For example, I am a huge tennis fan and I played it for decades. For most of that time I lived in northern cities and during the winter I had to join an indoor tennis facility and pay the membership and court fees. I signed up for groups that each played for two hours...at 7 PM on Monday and Wednesday. Sometimes after a long day at work I really wasn't in the mood to play two hours of tennis...but I did it anyway. How did I motivate myself to do it? I am basically a frugal (AKA cheap) person, and I intentionally paid my tennis court

bill in a lump sum on an annual basis. That meant that if I didn't go and play I would lose that money I had already paid...and I was too cheap to do that!

5. <u>Try to exercise with family or friends whose company you enjoy</u>, and hang around for a few minutes afterward to share some social time together. Sometimes the socialization is just as rewarding or even more rewarding than the exercise itself.

6. <u>Combine work and play if you can</u>. For example, I am a physician and to keep my state license I am required to get 60 hours of continuing medical education credit over a two year period. I joined the American Medical Tennis Association and went to their annual February event in a warm weather city (usually in Florida). This got me out of the cold northern weather for

a week, but also combined medical education and exercise. They had medical lectures from 8 AM to noon (for which I got continuing medical education credits), then had a quick lunch, followed by playing tennis all afternoon. Another example was a friend of mine who was a chemical salesman. He made most of his sales on the golf course, as many of his customers much preferred a free round of golf to a formal business meeting.

7. <u>Encourage yourself to exercise by making it a family event</u>. You obviously need to be spending time with your family, so why not do it with exercise? One of my fondest memories is back when my teenage son and I entered a tennis doubles tournament, and when my entire family entered a 5K run. Family events like this are fun, and more importantly help teach your children the importance of lifelong exer-

cise.

8. <u>Pick an exercise that you enjoy doing</u>. When you do an exercise you enjoy... you will look forward to it and not feel that it is a chore or a grind. This seems like an obvious rule, but I am amazed by how many people don't follow it.

9. <u>Cross training is good</u>. Instead of just doing one kind of exercise, it might be useful to pick two or three. Perhaps you could work out on a treadmill once a week, play a sport like tennis once a week, and take a bike ride once a week. This gives you options you can use for days when the weather is not suitable for one activity or the person you wanted to exercise with isn't available. I have a 79 year old friend that I take bike rides with two times per week. But he also does weight workouts at a local health club. If he weather is too bad

for bike riding, he just goes to the health club. Try to have options.

10. <u>Don't overthink which type of exercise you should do</u>...the important thing is to just do some exercise. Sometimes my patients ask me what exercise they should do, and usually I tell them to pick any exercise they are willing to do for the next few decades of their life. We could argue all day about the benefits of one exercise versus another...but the important thing is that we CHOOSE to actually do some type of exercise. In the words of Dr. William Bortz, exercise is critically important because: "If you don't use it, you lose it."

11. <u>Build exercise into your regular life</u>: Walk rather than drive to a destination less than one mile away. Ride a bike rather than drive to a destination less than five miles

away. When you go to the mall, park as far away from the entrance as you can. Always take the stairs, especially if you are only going up 1-2 floors. If you are physically able, mow your own lawn instead of hiring someone else to do it. There are many other examples of how you can build exercise into your "regular" life.

12. <u>As you get older, be flexible enough to change rather than discontinue your exercise program</u>. I have dramatically changed the type of exercise I do over the course of time due to aging. I played basketball until I was thirty, but elected to stop because of frequent injuries that interfered with my ability to make a living for my family. I played softball, especially church softball when I was in my teens and 20's, but I went on to other activities because of the seasonal nature of the sport and the difficulty of trying to find a suit-

able league. I have been a bicyclist since I mowed enough lawns to buy my first bicycle (a J.C. Higgins model from Sears and Roebuck that cost $19.95) when I was 14 years old. Bicycling is the most efficient form of human powered loco-motion, and I still ride a bicycle. But due to a lack of balance that came with age, I now ride a three-wheel racing bicycle and I have reduced my mileage to about 36 miles per week. I was an avid tennis player for decades, but had to give that up after rupturing the rotator cuff in my right shoulder and having to have it surgi-cally repaired. I was a runner for a couple of decades, until an unrelated knee injury required that I stop running. I substitut-ed more bicycling for the running. The overall message here is that as a physician I am promising you that almost regard-less of your physical condition, there is an exercise that is suitable for you, safe for you, and fun for you, even if you have to do it from a wheelchair. You just have to be motivated enough to look around and find it.

If I had known that I was going to live this long, I would have taken better care of myself. – Mickey Mantle

Suggestion #2: Never Stop Learning

Anyone who stops learning is old, whether at twenty or eighty. Anyone who keeps learning stays young. – Henry Ford

Let's say that your physician, like Rip van Winkle, fell asleep for 20 years and then woke up and resumed practice. Would you feel comfortable going to see that physician? Obviously not. I have been a physician for over 50 years, and the medicine I learned as a medical student is very different from the medicine being practiced today. How about if your physician was asleep for only five years...would you feel comfortable going to see him or her? I don't think I would be, because I know that medicine advances virtually every day.

As a physician I am required to get continuous training updates to keep my license. Most states require at least 25 hours of "continuing medical education" (CME) credits per year. This training is required on a regular basis now in many fields...including even the legal field. Most medical specialties now require that you take an examination every 3-10 years to maintain your "board certification." When I passed my board certification in my field when I was about 32 years old, it was a permanent certification. Medicine is so much more complicated now that it sparked a movement toward specialization and sub-specialization. I recently had one of my knees replaced by an orthopedist who operates only on knees. In medicine, as in many other fields today, you have to "know more and more about less and less" to be considered competent. When I graduated from medical school it was possible to take a one year internship and then go directly into practice as a general practitioner. Those days are gone. If you want to practice general medicine now you must complete a three year residency in Family Medicine or in General Internal Medicine.

Lifelong learning is critically important in most fields and professions because of rapid change in our society. These changes are not only new scientific developments, but changes in lifestyle, attitudes, and politics. I have adopted lifelong learning as a mantra...so much so that if I come to end of a day and I can't think of any new thing I learned that day...I am disappointed in myself. The new thing you learn each day doesn't have to be big...just something. It might not even be related to your profession...it might be that you learned a new way to improve your backhand in tennis, or a new way to make a tastier beef stew, or a new scientific fact, or a new theological insight.

One of the best ways to keep learning is to approach each day with a mind that is consciously open to new things. As a physician I have learned a lot from talking with patients. They come from all occupations and backgrounds, and often have insights or facts that I don't have. As Bill Nye the Science Guy once said: *Everyone you will ever meet knows something you don't.* I approach each patient as a learning experience. I had a medical instructor of mine decades ago who told me that each patient was a picket in my "picket fence of knowledge" that I needed to constantly improve my practice of medicine. He was right.

Keep an eye out for "associational" opportunities. I had an instructor in medical school who during his medical school training in the early 1920's got a job cleaning the plates in his medical school's bacteriology lab. He was told to be wary of the penicillin mold, because if it got on one of the agar plates it would kill whatever bacteria you were trying to grow. He told me that for two years he vigorously fought the penicillin mold and it never dawned on him once that you could grind up the penicillin mold and use it to kill bacteria in people. Thank goodness that in 1928 a Scottish physician named Alexander Fleming finally made this "association" and is credited with the discovery of use of penicillin as a medicine.

Another example...the CAT scanner. When computers came along we now had both x-ray machines and computers. I used both for years without realizing that they could be combined into an invention that would fundamentally change the practice of medicine. Fortunately an engineer in the UK by the name of Godfrey Hounsfield, working with a physicist Dr. Allan Cormack, was able to make this association and created the world's first commercially available CAT scanner in 1972. This story is even more amazing when you consider that when Hounsfield got the idea he was able to get his extensive research funded by the Beatles. The Beatles were making a ton of money with their music and invested some of it in Hounsfield's work. I suspect that the Beatles went on to make a ton more money from this invention. Medicine was changed forever, and Hounsfield won the Nobel Prize in medicine.

I could give numerous past examples of things that were sitting right in front of us every day and we just didn't make the connections and "associations." The key to discovering new things is not just to see them (all of us with normal vision can see them), but to "perceive" the associations that are possible. This ability to perceive is what "separates the men from the boys." One of the ways of being able to perceive rather than just see is to have a consciously open mind to new things, new knowledge, and new associations.

One way to constantly learn is to intentionally learn a new skill, especially if it involves doing something that you have always wanted to do. It could be a physical skill like learning to swim or learning to juggle. It could be something that could be turned into a job if necessary, such as learning how to repair bicycles or cars. It could also be a new sport. When my ex-wife and I were about 30 years old, we decided that one way to spend more time together would be for both of us to learn to play tennis. Tennis has the advantage that it only takes two people to play, and it can be a "lifelong" sport. She was nine months pregnant at the time and I was in a cast and using crutches because of a broken ankle. We waddled into an indoor tennis club in New Jersey and told the man at the desk that we wanted to learn how to play tennis. The man took a look at us and then turned and said to his partner in the back room..."Hey Bob...come out here. You've got to see this!" We hastily explained to him that we weren't intending to start for a few months.

Learning a new hobby can be useful now and extend well into your retirement. A hobby can just be a hobby, or it can develop into a business. If you go to the website Etsy.com you can see a lot of handmade products for sale from mom and pop businesses that most likely began as a hobby. I have friends who know a lot about a specific kind of antique car and own that car. They go to car shows and win prizes with their car, and constantly learn new things about it. You can learn to crochet or be a quilter, or learn how to make earrings. You can become an excellent baker or finally learn to play the guitar!

Another reason we need to keep learning is because the world is shrinking and becoming more competitive. Constant learning is one of the keys to making the new discoveries that will shape the 21st century. Some historians say that the 19th century was that of the United Kingdom, and the 20th century was that of the USA. It is too early to say which country will lead the 21st century, but without continuous learning we probably will not make the required best new discoveries. In that case collectively we and our nation will not be in a position to lead the 21st century.

Learn something new every day! Don't fall into the mistaken illusion that you are educated and knowledgeable enough already, and that no new learning is necessary. As the famous Wizard of Westwood UCLA basketball coach John Wooden once said: *It's what you learn after you know it all that counts.*

Suggestion #3. Be Willing to Risk Failure

Do not judge me by my successes, judge me by how many times I fell down and got back up again. – Nelson Mandela

It is rare for anyone to be an overnight success. Many successful people actually have a trail of failure behind them. An example of this is the author J. K. Rowling. Although she graduated from the University of Exeter, seven years later she ended up on welfare as a single mother, and considered herself a failure. She wrote her first Harry Potter book but couldn't get it published. Twelve publishers in a row turned her down. The

13th publishing house, Bloomsbury Press, finally bought the book. This occurred because an editor at Bloomsbury gave the first chapter of the book to his adolescent daughter, and after reading it she demanded to get the rest of the book. The first publishing of the book was only 5,600 copies. But the book was then taken on by an American publisher and the rest is history. She has created a $15 billion Harry Potter franchise around the world, and has a personal net worth estimated to be upwards of a billion dollars. She commented: *"It is impossible to live without failing at something, unless you live so cautiously that you might as well not have lived at all, in which case you have failed by default."*

It used to be that if a person failed in business that was pretty much the end of the game for them. They were typically labelled a loser for the rest of their lives. They usually couldn't get loans from banks or even their family or friends to start any new ventures. Since the penalty for failure was so high many people didn't start new ventures. The price of failure was just too high for them. The good news is that this situation has gradually improved over the years. These days those who try a new business that fails are no longer ostracized or labelled a loser, unless there was complete incompetence or criminal activity involved. People who fail are no longer locked up in a real or virtual debtor's prison. There is no definitive and permanent blot on their character or reputation. Today we should redefine failure, not as the failure to succeed in a venture, but as a Chinese Proverb said: *Failure is not falling down, but refusing to get up.* If you start a business and it is successful, then you win. But if you start a business that fails and you lose, you <u>learn</u>. As Henry Ford said after he went bankrupt before his success with the Ford Company: *Failure is simply the opportunity to begin again, this time more intelligently."*

Thomas Edison and his employees tried thousands of lightbulb filaments trying to find one that would burn for more than just a few minutes. All of them failed. He did not view this as a failure, however, because of the knowledge gained in the process. He said: *I have not failed, I've just found 10,000 ways that won't work.*

The fear of failure is still real, but an even bigger fear should be the fear of regret. If you succumb to the fear of failure and decide not to start a business venture that has some upside potential, you might spend the rest of your life regretting it. This is especially the case if later on someone else runs with the same business idea and makes a big success out of it. Hall of Fame basketball star Charles Barkley put it bluntly: *If you are afraid of failure, you don't deserve to be successful.*

I know that most of you, like myself, were not around in 1936 when Jerome Kern and Dorothy Fields wrote the well-known song *Pick yourself up, dust yourself off, and start all over again.* That is still a great bit of advice for us today. Keep in mind that they wrote this optimistic song in the depths of the Great Depression.

Each time you fail, you should learn what not to do in your next venture. One of the ways you can increase your chances of being successful is to be a person who gives solutions, rather than just complaints. In business you have to be constantly aware of your customers' complaints. But knowing the complaints is only part of the job. The most important part of the job is to come up practical solutions for the complaints. Whether you are the boss or way down the corporate ladder, a key to being successful and promotable is to develop a reputation for being a person with solutions, not just complaints. Sometimes bosses will force you to think of solutions. Back when I ran a large hospital I would often have people come to my office who were bitterly complaining about some aspect of our organization. I quickly learned that one of the best ways of handling such a situation was to appoint them and others to be on a committee, whose only job was to recommend to me ways of fixing the problems causing them to be so upset.

One of the problems with having a venture that fails is that it makes it that much harder for you to believe in yourself. Believing in yourself is critical to the success of any new venture, and is the first step to having others believe in you. Henry Ford once said: *Whether you think you can or whether you think you can't...you're right.* In my experience those with entrepreneurial personalities seem to have an almost irrational self-confidence in themselves and their abilities.

One of the best examples of a person failing but not giving up was President Harry Truman. He tried but failed to succeed as a haberdasher. He lived in his mother in law's house most of his adult life. Yet he became the President of the United States, and was the last one to do so without the benefit of having a college degree.

Failure is success in progress. – Albert
Einstein

Suggestion #4: Be a Good Listener

We have two ears and one tongue so that we would listen more and talk less. – Diogenes

If we were supposed to talk more than listen, we would have two tongues and one ear. – Mark Twain

I admit that I'm a "big talker." As an extrovert who loves to talk, I will sometimes talk as long as anyone will listen. I was asked to give the sermon one Sunday morning at our church when the minister had to be out of town. After it was over I personally thought I had done a pretty good job on the sermon. While driving home from church that Sunday morning I asked my wife how she thought I had done. I thought she was going to say...great job! But she replied: "Well, you had a lot of good opportunities to stop." I was reminded of the Mark Twain quote: *Never miss a good chance to shut up!*

When I was in college I had a speech professor who wanted me to be a sports play-by play announcer, because she felt that I had the "gift of gab." She was visibly upset when I told her that I had chosen to become a physician rather than a sports announcer. I think I do have the gift of gab, and gab too much. Maybe the gift of gab is really the "curse" of gab.

One of the most common complaints that patients have about their physicians is that "My doctor just doesn't listen to me...he/she is in too much of a hurry!" When patients come to see me as their physician, my job is to find out what is bothering them and try to fix it. In medicine we call the first part of the history the "History of the Present Illness" or HOPI. I have learned over the years that carefully listening to what they say about what is bothering them is critical to my being able to make a diagnosis and to ultimately help them. If I cut the interview short and don't listen to them fully I often can't figure out exactly what is bothering them. Many times the history is so critical that if I can't make a diagnosis after the history, the physical examination and x-rays and lab tests might not help very much. This is especially the case with something like the common and complex problem of low back pain. I need to know when it started, is it new or recurrent, was there any trauma, exactly where the pain is, is it accompanied by any bowel and bladder problems, is there any weakness or numbness in their legs or feet, have they had any kind of infection lately, have they found anything that helps it, what body position is the most painful, and many more questions.

It took me about a decade of medical practice to finally learn to ask brief questions and then listen carefully to the answers. This process of listening takes time, especially with elderly patients (like myself) who can have a lot of co-morbidities and often have difficulty expressing themselves. Listening takes time, and insurance companies don't want to pay for all this time. Sometimes I am forced to cut off the conversation and make decisions about their diagnosis and treatment. But that is a risky proposition. I once had a patient who had neck pain. I quickly asked her the usual questions, and just came up with the diagnosis of some type of neck "strain." I gave her the usual treatments, but she did not improve. At the next visit I asked more questions about her neck pain. It turns out that the pain only occurred about 4 PM Monday through Friday when her boss would come into her cubicle at work and stand behind her and berate her for the alleged poor quality of her work that day. I finally realized that her boss was her "pain in the neck."

Another important fact about listening is that it is critical to learning. As the Dalai Lama once said, *When you talk, you are only repeating what you already know. But if you listen, you may learn something new.* It is very unlikely that you can learn by talking. You can't learn if you prevent others from talking by dominating the conversation. You also can't learn if you "sort of listen." This situation occurs when you pretend to listen, but what you actually doing is taking the time they are talking to think about what you are going to say next. This is particularly the case when a person has "pressure speech." This occurs when the need to speak is so great that the person talks non-stop, so much so that it seems as if there is some pneumatic pressure in their head forcing out speech. If you really want to learn, be quiet and listen. As President Lyndon

B. Johnson once said: *If you're not listening, you're not learning.*

Learning is also critical to being successful in life. Those of you in the military recognize this as being literally true. It is unusual these days, for example, for an Army officer to advance to the rank of Colonel or General without a college degree and at least one advanced degree. As Bernard Baruch said: *Most of the successful people I've known are the ones who do more listening than talking.* Or as this anonymous quote says: *Listen thrice. Think twice. Speak once.*

Listening can also greatly help our fellow man. Christians in particular have a duty to love. As Christian theologian Paul Tillich once said: *The first duty of love is to listen.* Some people just need to "talk it out." Regardless of what is bothering them, it can help them if you just listen to them and let them "get it off their chest." There is an anonymous saying that: *Listening is one of the loudest forms of kindness.* Mental health professionals call this "talk therapy." Perhaps most mental health counseling in this country revolves around talk therapy. The therapist "hears them out" and then is often able to offer specific therapies or insights that could be helpful.

Listening is also a skill that, in addition to being "good manners", can add to your popularity as a person in your peer group. A person who is admired and respected and most likely to be voted "Prom King or Queen" is often someone who genuinely listens to their friends and others. They usually also have a sense of empathy, and the people talking to them can sense that. If you go around dominating conversations and not listening to what others have to say...don't be surprised if you are not voted "Class President." Don't talk about yourself all the time...it is not all about you. When a new acquaintance says "Tell me about yourself"...say "I'm really not that interesting...but I can't wait to hear all about you."

Listening is something that will not only help you, it will help those to whom you are listening.

If speaking is silver, then listening is gold. – Turkish Proverb

Suggestion #5: Keep Your Spousal Relationship Fresh

How to have a long and happy marriage is an age-old question. In the past, people didn't live as long as they do now. They could die from a host of things that are now just non-fatal conditions...like colds, flu, accidents, appendicitis, etc. In the "old days" most people didn't have to worry as much about divorce, because at least one of them was probably going to die soon anyway. I had a Catholic priest as a patient once who blamed the medical profession for the rise in divorce. He said that hundreds of years ago when we invented the phrase "till death do us part" death wasn't going to be take very long. He felt that these days if you pick out a spouse in your twenties, living with them until age eighty or ninety is probably just not possible for the great majority of people.

I feel, however, that our new longevity gives us the opportunity and the privilege of having long marriages, not the burden of doing so. I was at a 50th anniversary party for a couple once when the host told a joke that didn't get very many laughs. He said to the man of the couple, "50 years of marriage is quite a sentence...if you had shot her you would have gotten only 20."

One of the greatest challenges to marriage is that we live in an era of constant change. I have a relative by marriage who was born in 1900. He grew up on a farm using horses and buggies and kerosene lanterns. This relative lived until 1990. By the time he died he had seen the invention of automobiles, planes, computers, the atomic bomb, and we had been to the moon. He experienced more change in his lifetime than all of mankind has experienced since the invention of the wheel. This change is a problem for us and for our spousal relationships. We constantly have to adapt to change, or run the risk of being left behind. Five hundred years ago all a person had to do was copy whatever their parents did, because it probably wasn't going to change. But this insta-bility-producing change is accelerating and now one of the few "constants" in our modern lives is constant change.

I have noticed that human beings are not good at adapting to change, even when it is change for the better. The now constant change in our lives puts an extra stress not only on us, but on our spousal relationships as well. New inventions that cause paradigm shifts in our lives and lifestyles can seriously affect our marriages. With the advent of computers and cell phones, many jobs have be-come not just nine to five, but 24-7 experiences. People can now work from home, and can fall into the trap of working all the time. Spending all your time and energy at work can leave little energy and time for maintaining a marriage. One strategy for controlling this I have seen is to have a separate phone and computer for work. At five or 6 in the evening, turn off both your work phone and computer. Anyone contacting you will simply get a message that you are unavailable until 9AM or whenever you normally start your workday.

I believe that the more you know about your spouse, the easier it is to maintain a healthy spousal relationship. Men should know, at a minimum, the following things about their wives: birthday, favorite color, dress size, pants size, shoe size, ring size, pet peeves, favorite food, favorite restaurant, your children's birthdays, mother-in-law's birthday, what they like on a pizza, how they like their coffee, date of your anniversary, favorite activities, favorite things to do as a couple, what they want to be thanked for doing, and turn-ons and turn-offs. There are probably many more that you need to add to your specific list...take a moment to add your own "minimum things" to this list. I suspect that men can learn even more of these essential bits of knowledge and emotion that are needed in a relationship simply by watching any Hallmark TV movie, and observing how the leading woman in the movie reacts to various actions and emotions of the leading man in the movie.

What are the minimum things that a woman needs to know about her husband? Most women don't need a list because, in my experience, they are typically much more sensitive and tuned into these minimum things. Their list should include everything in the list above that a husband needs to know about his wife.

I postulate that it is good idea to also know about the personality characteristics of your spouse. I am fond of the Meyers-Briggs Personality Assessment. It looks at personality types in terms of how people perceive the world and make decisions. When my wife and I were in the process of getting married about 20 years ago, the minister marrying us insisted on some pre-marital counseling and had us take the Meyers-Briggs Personality Assessment. I learned some basic things about how my wife and I were similar and how we were different from a personality standpoint. I postulate that it is very helpful in the pre-marital setting because the couple is typically in that "love is blind" state that makes it difficult for them see any issues with their spouse-to-be that might be a problem in the future. Our minister postulated that much of our marital strife in the future would revolve around those differences in our personality traits. I suspect that psychologists and psychiatrists reading this would say that this testing is an over-simplification of the interpersonal human experience, and I suspect that in many ways they are right. But it has helped my marriage.

When you take the Meyers-Briggs you get a lot of data, including four "letters" that signify different personality dimensions. My wife and I had the same first three letters, but I was a J and she was a P. The minister explained to us that the J people tend to do things on time and are goal oriented. The P people tend to be procrastinators. That turned out to be absolutely true in our case. I am a person that if I have a paper or report due on Friday, I will turn it in by Wednesday. If you tell my wife to turn in a report or paper on Friday, she will ask you what time on Friday. If it is not due until 5 PM on Friday she might not start working on it until 4 PM. She is also a "90 percenter" in the sense that if she is doing a major thing like writing a book, she will do 90% of it and then set it aside. It might be weeks or months before she goes back to it and finishes it. This, of course, drives me crazy. She is a "deadliner" and to hold down the conflict that causes between us, she has granted me the power to give her an artificial deadline. If I need her to do something like take some books back to the library, I am allowed to give her a deadline by saying "please take these books back to the library before noon on Thursday." The moral here is that the more you know how your spouse thinks and acts the more likely you will be able to work together without creating conflict. It will help make working together a pleasureful relation-building experience.

I think it is true that opposites attract. This is great in the fog of falling in love...and being very different can create great strengths in a marriage. As I say elsewhere in this book, different personalities and skill sets can make the marriage stronger, as long as you recognize, admire and honor those differences. Someone once said that: "Opposites attract, until they finally kill each other." Don't let this be the case in your marriage. Everyone wants appreciation, so remember to appreciate the different gifts and skillsets in your spouse.

I think one of the most important things you need to do to have a successful marriage over a long period of time is to constantly notice and keep track of how your spouse is changing. I'm sure you are familiar with human development...a one year old is much different than a five year old. A 10 year old is much different from a 20 year old. Change in human physical status and personality continue throughout life. I think you will agree that a 30 year old is much different physically and personality wise than a 60 year old. The trick here is that you have to consciously observe these changes in your spouse as they occur over the course of time, and then then fall in love with that "new" person all over again. Otherwise you run the risk of waking up in bed a few years from now with a total stranger. The best way to keep in touch with where your spouse is in this development is constant communication...both talking and listening. There are some churches groups that offer marriage enrichment courses or events or weekends if you need a more structured type of communication.

Here are some "Be's" for you:

- Be there emotionally for your spouse,

especially at particularly stressful times, such as a new child in the family, death of your parents or grandparents, when a child leaves home, when you become empty nesters, when there is job loss or other sudden change, at a time of serious illness, etc.

- Be there physically as much as possible for your spouse. Sex is always better when it is mutually gratifying to both of you, so that both of you look forward to it.

- Be careful not to criticize or make fun of anything about your spouse that they can't change (height, eye color, lack of athletic ability, etc.).

- Be quick to get over marital tiffs. Don't hold a grudge. Try not to go to bed without working out a marital tiff. If you can't work it out by bedtime, try to tell your spouse something positive...like: "Let's work on this tomorrow when we are not so tired."

- Be very careful not to say anything negative about your spouse to your circle of friends. This often gets back to them and can cause marital friction. Remember that your spouse needs to feel that you respect her and appreciate her when you are talking to your friends. Complaining about your wife, for example, might seem like a macho thing to do when you are out "with the boys," but it almost never makes anyone (including your friends) respect you. Their real attitude is that you are a loser because you married a person whom you describe as a loser. I now make it a habit of praising my wife at work, in particular. Then when we have the annual Holiday party, my co-workers will walk up to my wife and say: "Your husband just can't stop talking about how great you are...what is your secret?"

• Be ever mindful that your primary "job" as a spouse is to help your husband or wife become the best, happiest and most successful person they can be.

Suggestion #6: Plan and Save for Retirement

Retirement is wonderful if you have two essentials — much to live on and much to live for. – Unknown

It has never been more important to save for retirement, or for whatever else you would like to do in your old age. Why?...because we are living longer and longer, so long that we can now actually "outlive" our money. For example, if you joined the military at age 18 as an enlisted man or woman, you could retire in 20 years. That would make you 38 years old. Since life expectancy in our country is now 76 years from birth, if this person died at age 76, he or she would spend almost twice as long in retirement as spent being employed. In 1935, when President Franklin D. Roosevelt signed Social Security into law, the life expectancy was 62 years. Since the retirement age stipulated in the Social Security legislation was 65, it was not expected that most Americans would even live long enough to collect it.

I suspect that retirement on a practical basis is a relatively recent concept. Life expectancy in Europe in the Middle Ages was 33 years of age. Life expectancy did not reach 60 years of age until the early 20th century. Of course there have always been individuals who have beaten the odds and lived a long life. Thomas Jefferson lived to be 83 years of age, and John Adams lived to be 91 years of age. (Curiously, they both died on the same day, July 4, 1826). In the past most people had a simple plan for their old age, they had a lot of children and hoped that at least one of them would take them in if they lived long enough for that to be necessary.

Most of us will live longer than the current life-expectancy age of 76. How is that statistically possible? The reason is that life expectancy tables include those who die in childhood. For example, I obviously survived childhood and at this writing I am 80 years old. This is already well past the normal life expectancy of 76 years. But using Social Security Administration's own actuarial life table[1] it is predicted that I will live to be 88.4 years of age. This table predicts that if you reach the age of 65, you have a likelihood of living an additional 18.1 years. This makes retirement even more of an issue, because if you live to the retirement age of 65, you have a likelihood of living a lot longer than just the 11 years predicted by the average life expectancy of 76 years. Genetics also plays a

---

1. https://www.ssa.gov/oact/STATS/table4c6. html

role here. My parents each lived to be 90, and had to live on their retirement income for 25 years. Genetics indicate that I will live just as long as they did. How long do the people in your family typically live?

As you read this keep in mind that being of retirement age doesn't mean that you have to "retire." I like to work, and I am only semi-retired. I agree with Catherine Pulsifer's quote: *Retirement, a time to do what you want to do, when you want to do it, where you want to do it and how you want to do it.* The work that I do now is what I want to do, when I want to do it, and how I want to do it. I have a number of part-time jobs, so if I lose one for any reason, I can "still keep the furniture."

We need to remember that retirement doesn't just affect us, but our spouse and extended family as well. We should plan for it and what we will do with all that available time. Ella Harris once said that: *A retired husband is often a wife's full-time job*. At the time of this writing I live in The Villages, Florida. It is the largest retirement community in the world, with approximately 150,000 elderly people. A brain surgeon recently retired to The Villages and had nothing to do but pester his wife all day. He didn't have any hobbies or sports that he liked. Finally his wife insisted that he get a job that would get him out of the house for at least a few hours a day...any job, even a minimum wage job. He got a job at one of the security gatehouses here in The Villages, his job being to open the gate and let residents drive into the community. During his training session, his instructor said: "Opening this gate is not brain surgery." To which the retired brain surgeon replied, "I know how to do brain surgery...what I need to know is how to open this gate."

The reason I am writing this chapter is to encourage you to make plans for retirement, especially a financial plan. Someone once said: "If you fail to plan, you plan to fail." I am not a certified financial planner, nor do I have any credentials to give you specific advice on how to invest your money for your future. I am just going to give you 10 personal caveats about investing for retirement. I haven't always done these things, so I can't claim that I have led by example in retirement planning. The following 10 caveats are things I have done or wished I had done.

1. **Start young**. There is a financial "rule of 72" which lets you calculate how long it will take you to double your money, based on the compound interest rate or other rate of return. For example, if you are getting a return of 10% on your investments, it will take you 7.2 years to double your money (72/10 = 7.2). When you start investing early, you have decades of years available for your money to grow by doubling multiple times. You will get much more retirement benefit from a $10,000 investment if you make it at 35 years of

age rather than at 60 years of age.

2. **Build up an emergency fund of half your annual income.** It is impossible to predict what will happen in the future, but you should at least recognize the possibility of bad things occurring like economic downturns, depressions, being laid off or being downsized from your job, pandemics, etc. You should be prepared to support yourself out of your savings for at least six months until you can get a suitable new job or even start your own company. One of the main advantages of this fund is that it means that you won't have to rob your retirement fund to get though a rough patch or lose your home or have your car repossessed .

3. **Try to work for a company or organization that puts its own money into your retirement fund.** Some

companies have a fixed income type of retirement plan. These companies or institutions carefully calculate how much money they have to put into their retirement fund annually in order in order to fund your fixed income retirement. Fixed income retirements are not as common as they used to be, but many hospitals and government agencies still give a fixed amount at retirement as long as you live. The US military, for example, gives you a retirement payment for life of approximately your base pay at the time of your retirement. You should talk to your employer and make sure you understand the requirements for getting "vested" in the retirement plan. Getting vested means becoming eligible for some or all retirement benefits. If the plan requires that you work there for a minimum of three years to get vested, keep in mind that if you leave before that time you will typically get nothing.

Most companies now prefer that employees use contributions to programs such as IRAs and a 401K plan for retirement. In these plans there is no guarantee of what your retirement benefit will be, it will vary depending on the total amount you and your company have contributed, as well as how well your investments performed. The best plans are the ones in which your employer matches some or all of your contribution to the 401K plan. The best plans are also the ones that are the most easily transferrable...since most Americans now work for multiple employers in their lives. It is generally a good rule of thumb that you should always maximize your contribution to IRA and 401K programs.

If you are self-employed, you have the opportunity to fund your own retirement plan. This is usually a "fixed contribution" plan, in which you decide to put a percentage of your income into a retirement plan, typically 10-20%. This means that you are managing the retirement fund investments, and how much money you have to retire on will be a function of how well you invest the money.

4. **Buy a house.** Buying a home is the most successful long term investment for most Americans. For many individuals the great majority of their net worth is the equity in their home. Unlike most anything else we buy, homes tend to go up in value over the course of time, especially over decades of time. Of course, the real estate market has dips along the way,

and sometimes homeowners find themselves "under water" in the sense that their home is not worth what they owe on it. But even in these situations the home value often recovers over the course of time. Keep in mind that homes require maintenance on a regular basis, from changing a light bulb to putting on a new roof. The home that I live in currently here in The Villages, Florida has doubled in value in the last nine years that I have owned it. I have owned many homes in my lifetime, buying and selling as needed when for employment reasons I moved from one part of the country to another. I have made money on some homes, and I have lost money on others. The ones I lost money on typically occurred when I bought a house and then tried to sell it in under a five year period. A couple of times I bought a house during a housing peak, and had to sell it during a housing downturn. But even when I lost money, I viewed it as a good investment because my family lived in a nice home, and if I hadn't owned the home, I would have had to pay rent. I considered the lost money just rent. I was also able to deduct the mortgage interest against my federal income tax.

5. **Live below your means.** It is very easy to borrow money these days, especially with credit cards. Having a small amount of debt can help support your credit rating (assuming you make the minimum payments as required on time). I suspect that the main problem is that we Americans have difficulty "delaying gratification." We want our new homes to be filled with new furniture and electronic gadgets. We want to drive a nice car rather than a jalopy. At the time of

this writing, most home-owner mortgage interest is tax deductible. But in most states, interest on other kinds of debt is not tax-deductible. Credit card companies can legally charge rather incredible interest rates, and the interest you pay could otherwise have been spent on improving your lifestyle or net worth or both. When my parents were young, they didn't expect to have a nice apartment or home that was fully equipped with modern appliances on the first day of their marriage. They worked for about the first thirty years of their marriage to achieve that. I suspect that couples today expect to live in a nice apartment or their own home that is fully equipped with modern appliances...on day one of their marriage.

If you want to stay out of debt, particularly credit card debt, learn to delay gratification. The fact that you want something right now, doesn't necessarily mean that you have to have it right now. Buying it a little later with cash rather than with a credit card will make you appreciate it even more. If you have $10,000 in credit card debt, you are living your life "$10,000 in advance," for which you will pay about 20% credit card interest. Warren Buffet, the famous investor, once said: *Do not save what is left after spending, but spend what is left after saving.*

Always keep an eye on your expenses. All business owners know that there are two basic ways of increasing profits. One way is to increase sales and revenue. The other way is to reduce expenses. One of the best techniques to help you live below your means is to keep an eye out for unnecessary expenses. One of the most successful businessmen in colonial America was Benjamin Franklin, who went from poverty to riches. He said: *Beware of little expenses. A small leak will sink a great ship.*

6. **Get professional assistance from a financial adviser.** Unless financial investments is a serious hobby of yours, you should get a real professional involved. This is especially true if you have a large amount invested in your retirement fund. If you own a company, it is likely that your employees will be included in your retirement investment plan. You have a fiduciary responsibility to make sure their money is invested well. Financial advisers typically know how to keep your retirement fund investments tax deferred, have strategies to maximize growth, and know the nitty-gritty details of local, state and

federal regulations that might have an impact on your retirement funds.

7. **Always know how your investment advisor is being paid.** There are a number of things you should know about your financial planner/investment adviser. One of the most important things is how they get paid. They certainly have a right to be compensated for their work and expertise, but you need to know how they are being paid. This varies widely. Some change a fixed rate, and tell you they will manage your fund for "X" dollars per year, regardless of how the fund performs. Others charge a rate based on your fund's size. They will tell you I will manage your fund for 1-2% of the total value of the fund. Some tell you there is no charge for running the fund, but they are entitled to commissions available when buying assets for your fund. There are many oth-

er models that are used, and sometimes mixed models are used.

The reason you want to know how your fund manager is paid, is because that will tend to tell you their incentives. If, for example, they are being paid by the commissions they get for buying assets for your fund, they might guide you toward "loaded" stocks or investments in real estate in which they earn a commission. Some stocks are "loaded" in that you have to pay a percentage of the stock value upfront just for owning that stock. It is my understanding that the "load" can be shared with the agent selling you the stock. This gives the fund manager an incentive to acquire assets for your fund that pays them, whether or not they are good investments for you. Also be aware of fund managers, who in some payment systems, are incentivized to "churn" your assets, rapidly buying and selling stocks. If your fund shows a lot of stock turnover, you should learn why this is occurring. Is it based on actually making money for the fund, or just making money for the fund adviser?

It is a good idea to do an annual assessment of your net worth. If it is not going up, why not. If one of the reasons for this is that your retirement fund is not growing as expected, compare its growth with the rate of return you would have gotten if you had simply invested it in an S&P or Dow Index Fund. You should also check with your friends who are similar to you in their life situation and inquire about their return on investment. If most of them are doing better than you, it might be time to have a different fund manager.

Another idea worth considering if you have a large retirement fund is to have an audit of it done at least every few years by an outside group not affiliated with your fund management company. This is a rare occurrence, but a number of years ago an orthopedist in a group practice was getting a divorce. His wife's divorce attorney did a deep dive on his assets, including his retirement fund. It turned out that the fund manager was spending all the money rather than investing it, and the receipts and reports the doctor was provided turned out to be bogus. This orthopedist and his entire practice group had no actual retirement funds. I don't know the end result in this case, but this could be a very big legal problem if the retirement fund also contained funds of company employees. You have a fiduciary responsibility to keep track of their money, and I suspect they could sue you for any of their money that was lost.

8. **Use a multiple pension strategy if possible.** I had a relative who retired from the Air Force with a pension. He then worked as a teacher in New Jersey for a number of years and became eligible for their pension. He also had a Social Security pension. He was able to retire on his Air Force pension, his savings, his New Jersey teachers' pension, and his Social Security. But wait...there's more. He married a woman who had also worked for the federal government. She retired on a federal pension and her Social Security. Between the two of them they retired on a total of five pension sources.

9. **Reduce your dependence on the Stock**

Market for investment as you get older. There is an old saying that your investment in the stock market should be 100% minus your age. At age thirty you might want to have 70% of your assets in the stock market because of the long upside potential. But when you are 70 years of age you might want to only have 30% of your assets in the stock market. This is because if the market takes a sudden dip, you don't have the decades of time left that it might take to recover.

One of the main problems incurred in retirement is progressive loss of buying power due to inflation for those of us on fixed retirement incomes. Inflation can cause you to outlive your retirement money really quickly. What would happen to you if a loaf of bread or a gallon of milk or a gallon of gas each cost $20? This is why you need to have some portion of your retirement income invested in things that are not fixed, but have upside potential. This is why some investment advisers recommend that we never get out of the stock market completely. The fact that Social Security payments are now indexed for the cost of living (COLA) has been very helpful for those who rely mainly on Social Security income for their retirement.

10. **Don't get divorced, especially if you are over 50 years of age.** In the states where I have lived your retirement fund might have your name on it, but it's really the property of both you and your spouse. Your spouse's divorce attorney will quickly point that out to you. I know that it is getting harder to stay married to the same person as we live longer and longer. Please see the chapter above in

that regard. But getting a divorce, especially after the age of 50, can be a disaster for your retirement dreams. In most cases, after a divorce you will end up with half your stuff, or at least what you considered to be "your stuff." That can set your retirement plan back decades. I have a physician friend who lost half of his retirement fund in a divorce. He then married a much younger woman, and in a few years got divorced. He again lost half his retirement fund...which left him with one-fourth of his original retirement fund. At the time of his second divorce he was 55 years old. Although he has a reasonably good income, he simply didn't have enough years left to rebuild the entire amount in his original retirement fund. I can only see two ways around this "divorce/retirement" problem. One way is to get some kind of pre-nuptial arrangement that might protect your retirement fund. You would have to check with an attorney in the state in which you live to determine if this is even legal. You would also have to get your fiancé to sign it. The second option is to always marry someone wealthier than you. Good luck with that.

The best way to avoid the disastrous consequences that divorce can bring to your retirement plan is to just stay married. I recommend that. Spend any amount of money necessary in marriage counseling or whatever else you need to do to stay married.

Because we now live so long it is likely that you will spend 20-40 years in retirement. Start planning for that now!

*Retirement at 65 is ridiculous. When
I was 65, I still had pimples.* – George
Burns

Suggestion #7: Be Trusting, but Don't be Gullible

There's a sucker born every minute. –
P.T. Barnum

I blame evolution. I believe that humans evolved over thousands of years under the direction of a supreme being. Traits that were an advantage in the fight for survival typically won out in the evolutionary process. Traits that were not an advantage tended to disappear over the course of time. I don't understand why people evolved in such a way that they can be gullible. What possible advantage would gullibility provide for survival?

One thing that comes to mind is that it might be an advantage for the survival of our species because of the "falling in love" process that occurs in dating and marriage. I think that women would have to be at least a little gullible to accept our hand in marriage. In the haze of falling in love, they apparently think we men are much better than we really are, and they appear to be under the impression that they can fix whatever minor faults we might have. As Oliver Hardy once said: *Well, if she was dumb enough to marry you, she'll believe anything.*

Today is a new and amplified era of gullibility. The internet and other modern forms of communication have made it much easier for us to be "taken in" because of this gullibility. A hundred years ago it was probably more difficult to be taken in because people back then weren't as overexposed to scammers, conspiracy theories and misinformation as we are now. It would seem that since most Americans these days have at least a high school education, gullibility would be less of a problem. But the internet by itself is much more powerful than in the "old days" when we could be taken in by a traveling snake oil salesman who tried to convince everyone that his new "miracle" patent medicine was a cure for just about everything. One of the tactics of these salesmen was to give out a few bottles of the miracle medicine for free to a few well-known people in town, and then later get their testimony on how well it was working for them. These otherwise honest people would say it was working well due to the "placebo effect" (see below)...and the fact that many of these medicines contained mostly alcohol.

As an octogenarian living in a retirement community I encounter criminal attempts to hoodwink me every day. These are much more convincing ones than the old "Nigerian prince" ruse. The elderly people in my neighborhood are constantly on the lookout for such fraudulent schemes (the elderly seem to be targeted by the scammers more than people of other ages). Despite our wariness, very intelligent people in my neighborhood are still gullible enough to be taken in by scammers from time to time. I am told that scamming people on the internet and on phone calls is a multi-billion dollar business.

Currently one of my part-time jobs is working at a "contract research center." This research center is owned by a company that is one of many in this country and throughout the world that contracts with "big pharma" to do phase I, II, and III studies of the new drugs that the companies want to get approved for sale by the FDA (US Food and Drug Administration). The FDA has a rigorous process for this approval, most of which is beyond the scope of this discussion. The FDA mainly wants the research presented to them to be controlled trials that are randomized and double-blinded. In this kind of trial subjects are recruited to try a new drug under the careful supervision of an Institutional Review Board, the company's research team, and the principal investigator physician at the contract research center. These research trials typically consist of giving the new drug to some subjects, and a medicine that looks like the real medicine but is mainly sugar or another inactive substance to those in the "control" group. Neither the subject or the doctor (or anyone else at the contract research center) knows whether the subject is actually getting the real drug or not. The subjects who are deemed as acceptable (meeting the criteria) for a study are randomized to get either the real drug or the placebo. Why go to this much trouble and expense? It is well known that if a subject feels that a medication is going to be helpful, there is a "placebo effect" in which they claim and actually feel that they are improved. We can control for this "placebo effect" by the fact that neither the subject or the research doctor know if they are actually getting the real drug.

If a study is not controlled in this way it is difficult to assess whether the new drug had any real benefit. I knew a doctor once who believed that penicillin could cure the common cold. He reported in one of his records that he had given penicillin to his last 100 patients with a common cold, and that all of them had recovered. We all know that virtually all patients with a common cold recover anyway, regardless of what medicine you do or do not give them. To see whether penicillin actually helped cure the common cold he would have had to do a research project in which a large number of patients with similar symptoms and characteristics were treated with penicillin or a placebo in a double-blinded manner. When the study was over, he would be able to break the code and prove whether penicillin made any difference in whether the patients recovered or not. By the way, for full disclosure, penicillin or other antibiotics can be helpful in some cases in which the common cold (which is a viral infection) progresses to a secondary bacterial infection. Keep in mind that the great majority of antibiotics are anti-bacterial only, and have no effect on viruses.

The sheer mass of misinformation that Americans are bombarded with, particularly on the internet, makes it more important than ever to "guard our gullibility" and not fall for this misinformation. The mere fact that something is on the internet does not necessarily mean that its true. The same can be said for books, magazines, television and newspapers. (For the younger people reading this, a newspaper is multiple sheets of large pieces of thin paper that are folded together and which have articles about the events of the day). Older people got used to reading the daily newspaper back before we had the internet, and we still like them...even though the ink often comes off on your fingers. But after you read them they have many additional uses, including wrapping up kitchen garbage or lining the bottom of a bird cage or being recycled.

I think being on "gullibility guard" is especially important in regard to health topics. As a physician and former medical school professor, I am sometimes absolutely amazed by the inane and inaccurate things I read about health on the internet. For example, there has been a large anti-vaccination campaign in our country before and throughout the Covid-19 pandemic. During this pandemic one million Americans died. This is about the same number of Americans who have died in all our wars from the Revolutionary War to the present. Unfortunately, many of these Covid-19 deaths occurred before we had a vaccine. But, overall, about 95% of the people have died from Covid-19 were not vaccinated. How many of them would have been saved if they had taken the vaccine? Some studies estimate that the death toll to date would have been 3 million lives without the vaccines. Over the past 2-3 years I have seen many people who survived Covid-19, but who were tragically left with life changing sequelae, including lung damage, nerve damage, and damage to other organs of the body. How much better it would have been for them if had simply taken the time to get vaccinated. The purpose of the vaccines was and is to prevent Covid-19 hospitalizations and deaths. The vaccines do not always prevent Covid-19. For example, even though I had taken the vaccine and multiple boosters, I still got Covid-19. But my case was a mild one. I recovered fully and did not have to be hospitalized.

Some have said that the risk of the vaccination's side effects are too high. Every vaccination has risks and possible side effects. I don't think it is possible to make any drug or vaccine that would have no potential side effects. I am fond of saying that if a medicine doesn't have any side effects, it probably doesn't have any effects at all. Also, virtually every medical decision involves a risk/benefit analysis. You have to ask yourself what do I have to gain by having this procedure or taking this drug, versus what do I have to lose. People are very different in their physical responses to medicines in general and to vaccines in particular. While the great majority might have only some arm pain or a mild local rash after a vaccination, it is possible to have a severe reaction and even death in a very small number of people.

Why didn't all of us get the Covid-19 vaccinations? Approximately one in five people in the USA at the time of this writing have not had any Covid-19 vaccinations. When I meet patients who have not had a Covid-19 immunization, I ask them in a non-judgmental way: Why not? Here are some of the reasons I have heard, in no particular order:

    1. They are anti-vaccine for any vaccination, and only get them when required by their job or school. Some refuse to get vaccinated even if threatened with job loss or having to home school their children. They have read "bad things" about vaccines and

don't want to have anything to do with them.

2. Some are not against all vaccines, just the Covid-19 ones. They sometimes can't articulate why they are refusing to have the vaccine, but just have a bad feeling about it.

3. They sometimes won't admit it, but it appears that some are just afraid of needles. I suspect that many of them will get vaccinated down the road if and when the vaccine becomes available in an oral or breathable form.

4. Some have a specific fear about the Covid-19 vaccines. One patient told me that she was afraid that it would cause sterility and she was trying to have children.

5. Some don't like the fact that the virus

keeps changing and over the course of time and becomes less sensitive to the available vaccines. They consider having to take the vaccine and then multiple boosters is too much of a wild goose chase. But the fact that the virus mutates and changes over the course of time is just a fact of life. Viruses and bacteria have the ability to have mutations that make them less sensitive or even completely resistant to our medications. This is one of the main reasons why boosters for Covid-19 are necessary...to keep up with the latest version of the virus. This is especially true of bacterial infections. For example, I remember a few decades ago when the Staphylococcus aureus bacterium became resistant to a type of penicillin called methicillin. This is known as methicillin resistant Staphylococcus aureus or MRSA. Many deaths occurred (including one of my relatives) until the drug companies were able to develop medicines that would kill this bacterium. This has resulted in a constant race between the antibiotic manufactures and almost all bacteria that commonly infect human beings. So the message here is don't be put off by the fact that the immunization you get right now might not work in 6-12 months.

How can you guard against gullibility in today's complicated and ever-changing world? Here are some suggestions for you.

1. <u>Get your knowledge from recognized and reputable sources</u>. The other day I heard one of my favorite comedians on a talk show say some very derogatory things about the concept of climate change, and intimated that those who believed in it were not all that smart. I know the topic of climate change is still controversial, but

my point here is that I am not going to get my information on climate change from one of my favorite comics. He is a comic genius, but he is not a climatologist or meteorologist, and does not hold any degree or advanced degree in a field relating to climate change. Getting your knowledge from a respected source is especially important on a health-related issue. Information gleaned from the websites of the Mayo Clinic or the Cleveland Clinic, for example, are inherently more reliable that taking health information from people on the internet who most likely have no credentials at all on the subject. These are people who have a right to their opinion and the right to put it on the internet, but they shouldn't be relied on in making health decisions for yourself or your family.

2. Check with others you trust before act-

ing on something on the internet that turns out to be a scam. This is especially good advice for the elderly. I remember when my father was about 85 years old, and still using a computer I had set him up with about a decade earlier. One day he called me and sounded very happy. "You're not going to believe this, but I just won the Irish Sweepstakes." He went on to say that he had gotten an email notifying him of this and that all he had to do to get the money was to send them his bank name and bank account number. I knew that my dad was very much against gambling, so I asked him if he had actually purchased a ticket for the Irish Sweepstakes. He readily admitted that he hadn't. Shortly after this it became obvious that he was developing Alzheimer's dementia and he asked me to take over his finances and bank account. A few months later he lost the cognitive ability to use his computer.

3. <u>If you get a phone call that could be a scam, just hang up.</u> For example, a common scam of the elderly is when they get a call that says that they will be arrested unless they pay a sum of money (usually $500 or more) to settle up a debt or some other obligation they haven't paid. They often can't remember whether they actually owe this money or not, but don't want to be arrested. Most scammers won't call you back, so if you just hang up they will go on to the next victim on their list. Another common scam is calling up an elderly person and claiming to be a relative, such as a grandchild, who has been arrested and needs a sum of money (usually $1000 or more) to make bail. Bank tellers are now sensitized to this and are suspicious when an elderly person comes

to the bank and wants to withdraw a large sum of money in cash. Again, just hang up.

4. <u>Do your own checking.</u> As a physician I recently had to go through the approval process to get my CAQH certification renewed. This is something that all physicians in the USA who send bills to insurance companies or Medicare have to have. CAQH is an acronym for a non-profit organization called the Council for Affordable Quality Healthcare. There are scammers pretending to be physicians who send false bills to insurance companies and demand payment. To prevent this from happening this system was developed so that when a doctor submits a bill to the insurance company, they can check the CAQH information and verify that the doctor is legitimate. The process of getting or renewing your CAQH certifi-

cation is done on-line. After renewing my CAQH certification recently, I got a call from a man who told me that there was now a new process in which they were following up by phone those who had recently renewed CAQH online...just to make sure of the legitimacy of the doctor. I talked to him for a few minutes and became more and more suspicious as he wanted me to give him personal information I had already given to CAQH online. I told him I was busy seeing patients (which I was) and hung up. I immediately emailed the CAQH people and asked if they were doing phone verification of the online information that I gave them. They said absolutely not and that this was a scam. So it doesn't matter how smart you think you might be or how many degrees you have, don't give up personal information on the phone or online unless you double check the authenticity of the person who wants that information.

5. <u>Get your news from multiple sources.</u> If you get your news only from one cable news channel, for example, you are at risk of adopting their biases and deepening your own. In their defense, I suspect that that cable news channels are under pressure to present the news in a way that their audience likes. They are under economic pressure to spin the news to please their listeners, otherwise they run the risk of losing their listeners. It is a good idea to get your news from multiple reliable sources, rather than relying on a single source. For example, on my phone I catch the headlines from the Indianapolis Star, the Philadelphia Inquirer, and the New York times. I watch the evening news on either ABC, CBS or NBC. I watch CNN, MSNBC, and occasionally Fox News. I

don't consider myself a news junkie...just a person who wants to be informed from various sources.

We all have to keep up our "gullibility guard," especially those of us who are older. Here are some examples of the more prominent scams or misinformation campaigns out there at the time of this writing:

- QANON, but this seems to be fading.

- Election Deniers, but this seems to be fading.

- False and unproven medications for Covid, but this seems to be fading.

- Many medications that are sold as supplements but which have not been tested in real research studies. These "medications" can be sold with wild claims with little or even no real supportive research. The reason for this is that under current federal law these "supplements" are exempt from having to go through an FDA approval process. Beware of any advertised medication that uses <u>testimonials from individuals</u> rather than real research to support its claims.

• Climate change due to hydrocarbon emissions is not real.

The good news is that "the truth will out." Over the course of time false information claims and conspiracy theories are slowly debunked. The problem is that this process takes time, and can be deadly...don't be misled by them in the meantime.

People seem to be awfully gullible. They'll believe anything. – Julia Child

Suggestion #8: Celebrate that America is Multiethnic, Multicultural, and Multireligious

S ome people are under the impression that our country used to be or is supposed to be purely Caucasian and Christian. Caucasian is a broad term, and most of the original immigrants to America were from virtually every nation in Europe and elsewhere. They were of many different religions, admittedly most of them Christian, including Puritan, Quaker, Baptist, Catholic, and many other denominations. Along the way we added the black people who were forced to come here against their will. Asians also came, most famously to help build the continental railway. There were also many Jewish settlers. Many Hispanic citizens were already here and became citizens when the areas they were living in became part of the USA. All of us, except for Native Americans, are immigrants.

At first glance, the American polyglot of peoples and languages and religions sounds like a recipe for chaos and disaster, but instead, it has produced the most powerful and most prosperous nation in the world. The danger is that we can easily devolve into "tribalism" and begin to hate everyone who is different from us. I firmly believe that our nation has greatly benefitted from all the different cultures, languages, and even the resulting genetic diversity. It might seem illogical, but I postulate that the more different we are, the stronger we are. Most Americans are hard-working, probably because our economic system of capitalism encourages it, but also because many of our ancestors who came as immigrants were motivated people who had the "gumption" to improve their lives and the lives of their families through hard work.

Diversity is common in other nations as well. There are 56 different ethnic groups in China, although the great majority are in the Han group. India has approximately 2,000 different ethnic groups, and so many different languages that citizens of India from different regions of the country can sometimes only talk to each other in English. The United Kingdom has dozens of ethnic groups that have immigrated from their former colonies.

Would a football team win many games if all the players were 350 pound offensive tackles? Obviously not. Football requires a diverse group of players and skill sets. The defensive backs and receivers have to have blazing speed. The quarterback has to have a strong throwing arm and the ability to find open receivers in just a few seconds. Some positions in football are hybrids. For example, a tight end is sort of a lineman, and also sort of a wide receiver. Diversity in physical attributes and skill sets appears to be the key to success in football.

I believe that diversity is the key to almost any successful enterprise. A corporation that manufactures a "widget" needs people who can get investors to fund their operation, and people who can design the widget, those who know how to manufacture the widget, and those with the skills to sell the widget. Most modern corporations require a wide range of employee skill sets to be successful.

It is my feeling that one of the reasons the USA has in the past been able to "hold it together" without devolving into tribalism has been our constitution. It is an old but living document, which when properly applied should give everyone an equal shot at what the Declaration of Independence calls the "pursuit of happiness." Unfortunately the constitution has never been fully applied to all our citizens, and is not even today...but

I hope and trust that we are moving in the right direction...when (as Martin Luther King said in his dream speech) people "...will be judged not by the color of their skin, but by the content of their character."

Here is a quick example of a diversity advantage for America. In World War II we used Navajo soldiers to send unbreakable messages in their language. Neither the Germans or the Japanese were able to break this code that was basically nothing more than the everyday language of the Navajo. This language was used because the government had determined that there were only 28 or fewer people who could speak this language that were not in the Navajo tribe.

Another quick example is the beauty of diversity in marriage. I have never been able to remember names very well, but fortunately I have a wife who can. Sometimes we will go to a party or other gathering and on the way home she will ask me: "What did you think of Roger?" I have, of course, no clue who Roger is since everyone I met is now a big blur in my mind. She can remember almost every name that she heard that evening. She can even remember who was married to who and what clothes they were wearing. "How about that dress Susan was wearing...did you recognize it?" It turned out that Susan was wearing a dress that my wife also owned, but in a different color. She helps me very much in awkward social situations with her naming ability. For example, once we were walking through a mall and met up with a couple who were acquaintances of ours. My wife knew I would not be able to come up with their names, so she started the conversation with "Dave and Barbara...how nice to see you again." At least I then knew they were Dave and Barbara. It works the other way as well. My wife is not vert good with math. So when any math situation comes up (even balancing the family checkbook) I usually end up doing it. Clearly we are stronger together than we are separately.

Here is another quick example of this. When my parents were older, my father lost most of his hearing and my mother became legally blind. The good news was that my father had excellent vision and my mother had very keen hearing. Between the two of them, they could see and hear. They were able to continue living in their own home much longer than I expected because of their ability to share each other's strengths.

Take a moment and think of examples of the advantages of diversity in your own life and family.

I've been thinking about why some "white" groups in our society appear these days to hate and want to control people who do not look like them. I first noticed this in the coal mining camp I grew up in (Monarch, Virginia) about 70 years ago. It was located in a "holler" bordered by mountains on three sides and had only one road in and the same road out. All of the local coal miners were white. They were intent on keeping African Americans out of the community. Looking back,

I postulate that the reason was mainly economic. These people had little education (most were not high school graduates), and had few actual job skills. Most of them were essentially manual laborers. I think they feared any group of people who might come to the area and be willing to do their work for less money. I suspect that they felt that this would severely disrupt their lifestyle and likely devastate their families.

In my search for the reasons for our national racism, I have come up with three basic reasons (I am sure academicians and social scientists have come up with many more). The first is that it seems to me that everyone has an inborn need to feel better than someone else. Poor and uneducated white persons could well find satisfaction in believing that regardless of how low their life station, they were innately better than Blacks or Asians, etc. When I got to college, I was taking difficult pre-med courses. One of my friends was a student from Nigeria (I won't give his name). He was incredibly smart. I took a physics course with him and he would sit in class and listen but not take very many notes. He would just occasionally nod his head and smile. He also didn't need to study very much. When the physics tests came around, we could count on him to be the first one to turn in his paper and pretty much always made the highest score. I had been brought up to believe that white people were innately smarter than black people...so much for that theory!

I was brought up to believe that Christian people were better than Jewish people. But how about this statistic...20% of the Nobel prizes given in the last 50 years have been won by Jewish people, even though they are less than 1% of the world's population. So much for Christian people being innately better than Jewish people.

My second reason for our national racism is that we tend to generalize when we don't like an individual who is not like us. There are individuals in a number of ethnic groups whom I personally don't like very much. But I have resisted the urge to generalize and say that I don't like anyone in that ethnic group. How easy it would be when I came across a black person I didn't like to say...those black people are all alike!

My third reason for our national racism is that we are moving slowly but surely to a time when white people will not be in the majority in our country. I am pretty sure that the far-right wing hate groups get very upset when non-whites are successful in our society, and particularly when they are successful in government. This success requires that they spend considerably more psychic energy convincing themselves that their core belief that white people are superior is still true. Their own inferiority complex is made worse when non-whites are successful. The election of President Obama, and the appointment of judges from non-white ethnic groups (especially to the Supreme Court), are recent examples that probably caused them to feel that non-white people were "taking over" and this trend had to be stopped. Currently whites in America outnumber all other groups combined, but that is slowly changing. William H Frey, a senior fellow at the Brookings Metro, has projected that whites in the USA will be in the minority by 2045. At that time he predicts that whites will be 49.7% of our population, Hispanics 24.6%, African Americans 13 .1%, Asians 7.9%, and Multiracial 3.8%. I suspect that many whites are worried about this because white people have always been in the majority in this country, going back to its founding. They fear that they and the entire white race will "lose control," due to the democratic notion of "one man one vote." So many of them try to make it hard for people of color to vote (I realize that this is nothing new and has been a common practice in our country, particularly in the South). Some far right wing groups are calling for an end to democracy and permanent "white rule." Some are saying that the concept of "one man one vote" is now out of date and we need limitations on who can vote. I admit that I am a bit of a "radical" on this issue of voting. I believe that voting is not just a right and privilege, but also a duty...like jury duty. I believe that people who don't vote should have to have a note from their doctor or else pay a fine. But that is just my opinion.

I grew up in a very loving home, but when I was a teenager I began to realize that my parents, like their parents, were racist in many ways. They led a schizophrenic life in which it was very important for them to take up offerings in church to support the work of Christian missionaries in Africa. Yet they did not really want black people in their church or even in their life. They were a product of the Jim Crow South and their racial views were shared by most of their friends (who were also from the South). This became very apparent when I announced during my junior year in college that my roommate the next semester would be black. They strenuously objected, and even threatened to withdraw any financial support they were giving me. I actually didn't need much financial support at that time because I had an almost full ride scholarship, had a job that covered my room and board and gave me a few dollars of spending money each week (waiting tables and washing dishes in a girls' dorm). Unfortunately, I succumbed to the parental pressure and told my friend that I could not be his roommate. He went on to accomplish many great things in life, and when I met up with him at our 50th class reunion I again apologized profusely to him, but I could tell that he still had not been able to fully forgive me.

I am proud to say that as my parents got older they started to realize that their views were racist. They changed rather dramatically and even welcomed black people into their fundamentalist church. I wish I could say that I was the reason my parents changed, since I did nag them about it from time to time for years. But I think the real reason might have been the television show by Norman Lear called "All in the Family." My parents loved that show and faithfully watched it every week. I think at first they liked the lead character Archie Bunker, probably because he would say things about race that they believed but were too timid to say out loud. But my parents were very intelligent people and I think they ultimately realized that Archie Bunker was a flawed character who had hate in his heart.

I knew my dad in particular had it in him to change, especially when during my pre-teen years a distant relative wearing a KKK ring showed up while we were visiting my grandparents in Cookeville, Tennessee. Dad verbally went after this guy in a way I had never seen him do before or afterward. This distant relative and Archie Bunker were not following the words of Jesus when Jesus said that we have to love everyone, especially our enemies.

I suspect that every race and ethnic group has at least a small modicum of racist feeling and possibly even racist instinct. Even those of us who try every day not to be racist can still have some racism at the core of our subconscious mind. Here is my own method to test your own level of inner racism. If you are a white person and you feel anxious or flushed or start to sweat when you see an inter-racial couple...ask yourself why that happened. In your conscious mind you might have long ago accepted that everyone should be able to date and marry whoever they feel is the right one for them. But you are having an autonomic reaction anyway. Could it be that down in your subconscious mind you still have a problem with inter-racial marriage and that is causing you to be involuntarily anxious or sweaty or emotionally upset? Another example is if you have an autonomic reaction if you see a gay or lesbian couple holding hands or having a public display of affection. Another example is if you are a male of any color and you have anxiety about having a female minister or rabbi, or a female boss at work.

To those who are fearful of living in a country where people of color are in the majority, I say to you: Trust the Constitution. Trust your democratic institutions, like the Internal Revenue Service (yes, even the IRS), the courts, the military, Congress, the FBI, etc. Our governmental institutions are certainly not perfect, so it is important to continue to work on improving them. But even if we have a part of government that we think needs revision and updating, we shouldn't "throw the baby out with the bathwater." We must defend the Constitution against all enemies, both foreign and domestic. Otherwise we run the risk of devolving into the autocracy that we fought so hard to defeat in the 1770's and which we have fought against in multiple wars ever since.

By the way, if you haven't already read it, I suggest that you re-discover what a thin layer of civilization we have by reading *Lord of the Flies* by William Golding.

The greatest and noblest pleasure which men can have in this world is to discover new truths; and the next is to shake off old prejudices. – Frederick the Great

Suggestion #9: Don't Join Organizations that Discriminate

No one is born hating another person because of the colour of his skin, or his background, or his religion. People must learn to hate, and if they can learn to hate, they can be taught to love, for love comes more naturally to the human heart than its opposite. – Nelson Mandela

You were probably as shocked as I was when I learned that the Taliban, who now run Afghanistan, have recently begun preventing girls from attending middle school and high school. Girls are now allowed to go only to the sixth grade. There is a tendency is many religions to limit what women can do. In the Roman Catholic church women cannot become priests or be in line to be the pope. In the Southern Baptist church women cannot be deacons or ministers. In the Presbyterian Church in America (the second largest group of Presbyterians in the US) women cannot be ministers, deacons, or elders. They also cannot teach men. I could give many additional examples of religions that limit the roles of women in life, as well as in the church or synagogue or mosque.

I grew up in the Southern Baptist church, the second largest denomination in the USA (second only to Roman Catholicism). My parents and my church were both very fundamental. They believed that the Bible had to be interpreted literally. In their view, God actually did create the world in seven days. Women were actually created from a rib of Adam. Women could not be deacons or ministers. I have many fond memories of growing up in this denomination. The people were for the most part warm and loving and were true believers. The great majority of them were not hypocrites...they "talked the talk," but they also "walked the walk." I guess you could say that I am now a "recovering Southern Baptist." Since that time I have been a member of churches in a number of protestant denominations. My career path led me to move from time to time from one city to another. After each move, I searched the local area for a church that would be nurturing, especially for my children. I was not "brand-specific," which means that I was willing to join a church of any mainstream Christian denomination. This led me over the course of time to be a member of churches that were American Baptist, Church of Christ, United Methodist, and the Presbyterian Church USA.

Over the course of my life I have become more theologically liberal. I am proud of that, because I think that most people tend to become more conservative as they age. I suspect that it is "normal" to get more conservative with age, but I have never aspired to just be "normal." I have to be upfront with you, I am a believing Christian. I am also evangelistic about it...not "in your face" evangelistic, but if you have any interest I would be happy to share the message of Christ with you. I sincerely believe that in a free country everyone has the right be to any religion they want, or to be no religion. I am definitely not a fundamentalist anymore. I don't believe that story in Genesis about how the world was created is literally true...but that it is a wonderful extended metaphor about the role of God in our creation and in our lives.

I also believe that Christians over the course of the centuries have tended to confuse the message of Jesus with the traditions of the first century. My dad was the greatest man I have ever known. He was the most devout and least hypocritical person I have ever met, and his goal in life was to be a "First Century Christian." That was never my goal. My goal is to be a "21st century Christian." The message of Christ...a message of love for God, and love and tolerance for all mankind...can be easily lost if it is mixed with first century cultural beliefs, practices and prejudices. I call this "Christian First Century-ism." The first century was a terrible century. Jewish women, for example, had essentially no rights...they couldn't own property and didn't even own their own children. They had few, if any, leadership rights or opportunities. Their education was usually even sketchier than that of their husbands. The rights of women in other cultures in the first century were typically not much better.

Just because Jesus came in the first century doesn't mean that we have to live like it is still the first century. Somehow these terrible first century cultural conditions for women became part and parcel of Christian teaching. Jesus didn't tell us to do this. Read just the verses spoken by Jesus in the

New Testament (in some Bibles the words of Jesus are in red letters). Jesus never told us to discriminate against women, or anybody else for that matter. Over the centuries women were taught to act like Paul instructed in First Corinthians 14:34-35 that *Women should keep silent in the churches. For they are not permitted to speak, but should be in submission, as the Law also says.* He went on to say in I Timothy 2:11-12: *Let a woman learn in silence with full submission. I permit no woman to teach or to have authority over a man; she is to keep silent.* Paul told married women in Ephesians 5:24: *Wives should obey their husbands in everything, just as the church people obey Christ.*

I suspect that most of you have thankfully come around to the viewpoint that marriage is an equal partnership, not a dictatorship. In fundamental protestant churches, however, married men are told that have to be the head of their household. My parents openly and vigorously espoused that viewpoint, but the truth of the matter is that my mother ran our family in every sense of the word. She even picked out the clothes my father wore each day. Not all fundamentalists agree with this paternalistic view of marriage. A radio preacher I used to listen to when I was growing up in Dayton, Ohio, the Reverend Kash D. Amburgy, once said: "You can't trust a man who says he runs his own family...a man like that will lie about other things."

I suspect you have figured out by now that the Apostle Paul wasn't married. Why would he say these things to women? If you made comments like these about women openly at your job in any major company in the US, I suspect that you would be called into human resources before the day was done. In these verses Paul is inserting the first century worldview of women that he had experienced and had probably been taught during his rabbinical training in the early part of the first century. I suspect that his reason for writing these verses was that he was first and foremost an evangelist...and the best one Christianity has ever had. He went on at least three missionary journeys on foot and by boat that covered much of the known world at that time. One of the "problems" for the early Christian church was when women became Christians, they had a new-found freedom in Christ. They apparently began to go without head coverings, and to speak in public, especially in Christian services. It was likely back then that the only Jewish women who spoke openly in public were prostitutes. Paul probably felt that freedom for women was "turning off" some potential converts, perhaps men in general and Jewish men in particular. I think he was asking women to act in a way that wouldn't scare off potential converts. If he was giving advice to woman today I suspect that he would advise them not to dress or do anything so far out of the norm that it would be "weird" and scare off converts. But I suspect that Paul's best advice to women today would be not to give them any advice, except the advice to all of us that we shouldn't act in such a way that it turns off or scares away possible converts to Christianity. Paul practiced that in his own ministry. He tailored his message to each group or nationality as he said in I Corinthians 9:22: *To the weak I became weak, to win the weak. I have become all things to all people so that by all possible means I might save some.*

It should be kept in mind that Paul praised his women colleagues like Priscilla and Lydia for their leadership in the early church, so much so that he seemed to be a little schizophrenic in his view of women, especially in regard to Jewish law. In this verse he drew on Jewish law to justify his feeling that women should be quiet and in submission: *Women should keep silent in the churches. For they are not permitted to speak, but should be in submission, as the Law also says* (I Corinthians 14:34-35). This is odd because Paul preached that the message of Jesus brought freedom from the law, and the Mosaic law had been replaced by the simple law of Christian love. Here are a few of verses in which Paul said that:

- Romans 6:14: *For sin shall not be master over you, for you are not under law but under grace.*

- Romans 10:4: *For Christ is the end of the law for righteousness to everyone who believes.*

- Galatians 3:13: *Christ redeemed us from the curse of the law, having become a curse for us...*

- Galatians 5:1: *It was for freedom that Christ set us free, therefore keep standing firm and do not be subject again to a yoke of slavery.*

- II Corinthians 3:3: *...being manifested that you are a letter of Christ, cared for by us, written not with ink but with the Spirit of the living God, not on tablets of stone but* *on tablets of human hearts.*

Let's face it! In the 21st century we know that men and women are equal. Men and women are certainly different. For example, most men are physically stronger than most women, but most women live longer than men, etc. Don't be a member of the Christian Taliban! Let's treat women as equals and respect them as such.

Now let's turn our attention to discrimination occurring to individuals who self-identify as "LGBTQIA+." Here is what the letters mean (although this acronym changes from time to time and there is still not universal agreement about what each letter means):

L = Lesbian (Usually applied to women and girls). These are women who identify as females and who are attracted to other females

G = Gay (This can be a catchall term, but is now usually applied only to men and boys). These are individuals who identify as male, and who are attracted to other males.

B = Bisexual Applied who those attracted to both sexes.

T + Transgender Applied to those whose gender identity differs from what they were assigned at birth. Some go through surgery and hormonal treatment to become more in keeping with the gender with which they identify.

Q = Queer or questioning. Queer means everything on the spectrum of human sexuality that is non-straight and/or non-cisgender. Questioning is used by those to whom more than one letter applies, or their identity is more in a gray area.

I = Intersex. These individuals (about 1% of births) have sex characteristics, including genitals, that fall outside of the traditional conceptions of male or female bodies. Typically a gender is assigned by doctors or the family at birth. The individual might or might not have surgery and hormone treatment to become more like one gender or the other.

A = Asexual. These are generally non-sexual individuals, but there is a spectrum of these.

+ = Everything else. Sexuality and gender are a spectrum, and additional kinds with their own letter are yet to be named.

The Bible (both in the Old and New Testaments) has nothing nice to say about homosexuality. The ancients didn't understand it, and certainly didn't like it. Christianity and some other religions hated homosexuality so much that to be identified as homosexual could cause you to be killed. For those who interpret the Bible literally, these anti-homosexual verses are bluntly stated and hard to ignore. There is still widespread discrimination in Christianity against homosexuals or anyone in the LGBQTIA+ spectrum. This is seen is other religions as well. This is another example of how "first century-ism" colors our theology. I know of a group of about twenty lesbian women in my community who are devout Christians, but who do not feel comfortable in local churches. They have, at times, resorted to meeting in their own group as an informal church. One of them told me that she had tried to go to a local mainstream protestant church. She was honest with the pastor about being a lesbian. He told her that he couldn't prevent her from attending his church, but that he wished that she wouldn't. So much for Christian love!

Homosexuality has been around for a long time. Many famous historical figures were gay, including Oscar Wilde, Bayard Rustin, Lord Byron, Sir Francis Bacon, Leonardo Da Vinci, Aristotle, and many more. Some of currently famous individuals who are gay include Jay Leno. Rachel Maddow, Ellen DeGeneres, Anderson Cooper, Tim Cook, Robin Roberts, Elton John and many others. We know a lot more about the gender spectrum and homosexuality now than we did in Biblical days. We now know that you can't "catch it." You are essentially "born that way." Some parents don't want gay teachers in schools because they are falsely convinced that these teachers can somehow cause their children to "catch it" and be homosexuals as well.

The American Psychiatric Association (APA) removed homosexuality from its list of mental illnesses in 1973. In 1994 the APA stated that: "...homosexuality is not a matter of individual choice" and that research "...suggests that the homosexual orientation is in place very early in the life cycle, possibly even before birth." Many Americans mistakenly feel that homosexuality is a conscious choice, and that gay people could voluntarily decide to be heterosexual. The American Academy of Pediatrics stated in 1993 (reaffirmed in 2004) that "Homosexuality has existed in most societies for as long as recorded descriptions of sexual beliefs and practices have been available," and that "Most scholars in the field state that one's sexual orientation is not a choice ... individuals do not choose to be homosexual or heterosexual."

There are many other myths that circulate among anti-gay activists. For a list of some of them, I recommend the article 10 Anti-Gay Myths Debunked | Southern Poverty Law Center (splcenter.org) from the Southern Poverty Law Center.

For some reason Americans overestimate the percentage of gay or lesbian people in our society. A Gallup Poll in 2002, for example, asked Americans to estimate the proportion of men and women who are gay or lesbian. The result was an estimate of 22% of women and 21% of men[1].

The actual number (there have been a large number of studies and polls in this regard) is about 5% or less. Many Americans feel that the number of gay people is increasing. I suspect that this is not due to an actual increase in the real

---

1. https://news.gallup.com/poll/259571/americans-greatly-overestimate-gay-population.aspx

number, but due to more gay people now being "out of the closet" and willing to state that they are homosexual.

As noted above, the continued hate of homosexuals and all of those who are LGBTQIA+ in churches is unfortunately another example of "first-century-ism" contaminating our Christian theology. Again, read the "red letters" in the New Testament. Jesus never spoke about homosexuality. Look it up!

It seems to me that we are now in a situation in which many of our country's laws and practices have advanced from an ethical standpoint to a higher level than the tenets and practices of many of our churches. We have federal laws in particular that make it illegal to discriminate against women and gay individuals. For example, if I were to stand up in a group of employees of a large business and say that women should not be allowed to occupy any position of leadership, and that gay people should not be hired...my career in that company might be over. But if that same person would stand up in many of our churches and say the same thing, he would likely get an "Amen."

Now let's turn our attention to discrimination and hate against Jewish people. Jewish people are among our most productive citizens. They truly help make our country great! I have tried for years to try to understand why there have been centuries of discrimination and hate for jews...which continues today in our country, and which appears to be even be on the upswing lately. I suspect that the first reason for anti-Semitic hate is that people generally seem to fear groups who are different from them. Differences cause fear, which then becomes hate. Another reason is that many in our country seem to have a need to feel better than someone else. Sometimes their own life is so disappointing that is hard for them to find anyone they feel better than...so they pick a whole class of people to hate...in this case Jewish people. Another reason I suspect is that they are simply jealous of them. Jewish people are typically smart, hard-working, and successful in whatever they do. This is particularly a problem for those who are in relative poverty or who are undereducated, or who feel dispossessed by society. It could be that this situation makes people "prejudice prone." They start to irrationally blame Jewish people for national problems and for their own situation in particular.

You might not be familiar with one of my favorite stories in American history from the time of the revolutionary war. Haim Salomon (1740-1785) was a Polish Sephardic Jew who was a critically important force in the financing of the revolutionary war. He was a multilingual financier who came to this country in 1770, and in 1776 joined the New York branch of the Sons of Liberty. He was arrested twice by the British, and sentenced to death the second time, but escaped and moved to Philadelphia. Once in Philadelphia he became the agent to the French Consul and was paymaster for French forces in North America. In 1781 he began working extensively with Robert Morris, the Superintendent for Finance for the Thirteen Colonies. In August of 1781 General Washington and the French Navy had a chance to trap British General Cornwallis' forces at York-town. Washington planned to march his troops to Yorktown, but had no money and the troops were near mutiny because of lack of payment, uni-forms, food and supplies. Washington estimated he would need $20,000 dollars to get to Yorktown and fight the British. This was critically important because the surrender of all British forces at York-town, and the resulting Treaty of Paris in 1783 gave us our independence. Washington apparent-ly was told by Superintendent of Finance Robert Morris that there was no money and no credit and no way to raise $20,000 (this would obviously be a much larger sum in today's dollars). Wash-ington insisted he get Salomon involved. Prior to this Salomon already had a record of either raising or donating over $21 million dollars (in today's dollars) for the war effort. Salomon was able to get the $20,000 Washington needed, and the rest is history.

When you travel the world, you will notice that American culture seems to be evidenced everywhere. This is true in all kinds of businesses and especially in show business. American movies are beloved all over the world. Jewish people have made a huge contribution to US business, especially to the US entertainment industry. These contributors include visionaries like Disney and Spielberg; comedians like Groucho Marx and Jerry Seinfeld; movie stars like Steven Seagal and Carrie Fisher, singers like Barbra Streisand and Billy Joel; and the list goes on seemingly infinitely. I didn't realize how much American movies are popular all over the world until I was on a trip to China a couple of decades ago. The guide for our group was a wonderful young Chinese woman who led our sight-seeing activities. She spoke perfect American English...so much so that I asked her if she had spent time as a student in the US. She told me that she and her fellow guides were taught to speak American English by studying and repeating the dialogue of American movies. She then smiled at me and said in her best Clint Eastwood voice: "Make my day!"

Another reason by Christians are often antisemitic is the old and now debunked theological notion that the Jews were responsible for the death of Jesus. There were pogroms against Jews in Russia after the Christians began calling the Jews "Christ Killers." Keep in mind that Jesus was Jewish. I am fond of the bumper sticker that some Christians have on their cars that says: "I work for a Jewish carpenter." Christians should know that while Jewish elements agitated for the death of Jesus, they did not have the political power to actually do it. Some of the Roman leaders were actually ones who killed Jesus. Christians should also know that the death of Jesus and his subsequent resurrection after three days was pre-ordained and foretold by the ancient prophets. The idea that Jewish people should have a collective guilt for the death of Jesus was formally disowned by the Roman Catholic Church at the Second Vatican Council in 1965. Pope Benedict subsequently extensively delineated the theological basis for this in his book: *Jesus of Nazareth, Part II.*

This nation is replete with Jewish charitable (not for profit) institutions like hospitals and universities. Jewish people have given this country much, and they should be honored and respected for it. I have seen their charitable work first-hand. For a couple of years I was the Vice President of Medical Affairs at MossRehab, a Jewish rehabilitation hospital in Philadelphia. I worked with about thirty board members, I think all of whom were Jewish. They hired me to do this job even though they knew I was not Jewish. These board members were all successful people in their own fields and they were very proud of MossRehab, which began in the early 1900's and pioneered in the development of teams of medical professionals who developed special techniques to treat individuals with brain injury, spinal cord injury, stroke, amputations, multiple trauma, and other devastating physical impairments. The board members had a deep commitment to giving back to all Americans, so that others might benefit from whatever success they might have had in life. The board worked diligently to raise and to donate the money needed to make sure the hospital always had outstanding staff and administrators so that the good work of MossRehab could continue. MossRehab continues to this day to be one of the best rehabilitation centers not only in the USA, but in the entire world.

Out of 350 million Americans, only about 7.3 million are Jewish (about 2%). How can only 2% of our population have and continue to accomplish so much? We shouldn't be prejudiced against them, we should emulate them...whatever they are doing...it's working for them and for our nation!

You have choices in this country and responsibilities in regard to organizations you join. I believe that as a Christian you should not join any organization that has discriminatory policies against women or gays or Jews or people of color or anyone else. Stand up for women's rights and gay rights! Don't join or support organizations that discriminate against them. Stand up for the rights of all religions and races and ethnic groups! Let's follow the teaching of Jesus that we should love rather than hate everyone, even our enemies:

But to you who are listening, I say: Love your enemies, do good to those who hate you, bless those who curse you, pray for those who mistreat you. If someone slaps you on the cheek, turn to them the other also. If someone takes your coat, do not withhold your shirt from them. Give to everyone who asks you, and if anyone takes what belongs to you, do not demand it back. Do to others as you would have them do to you. Luke 6:27-31.

There is an old song that says "They will know we are Christians by our love." Let's all endeavor to be more Christ-like.

I don't reject Christ. I love Christ. It's just that so many of you Christians are so unlike Christ. – Mahatma Gandhi

Suggestion #10: View Change as an Opportunity

There is nothing permanent except change. – Heraclitus

No group of humans has ever encountered as much change in their lives as we have. A couple living in, for example, the tenth century had much less change to deal with in their lives. They basically learned the skills they needed to survive just by watching and copying their parents. Their children then learned the same skills from them. Not much changed. Occasionally in human history something comes along that causes massive change, such as the invention of the wheel, or the discovery of how to make iron products. But change in the "olde days" typically happened at a slow and manageable pace.

A person born in the year 1900 in the USA, and who lived to be 90 years old, probably experienced more change in their lives than all of humanity up until that point. They were born at a time when transportation was by horse, light sources were candles and kerosene lamps, and heating their home was mainly by wood-burning stoves. Think of how many things they experienced and had to adapt to by the time they died in 1990. Some of these things included the car, the airplane, space travel, computers, air conditioning, modern home appliances, amazing advances in medicine, and I'm sure you can think of many more. (By the way, the favorite change in my lifetime has been the invention of suitcases with wheels).

The rate of change is accelerating. Sometimes it seems like the only constant in our lives is that things constantly change. We have to adapt to this ever increasing rate of change in many ways. An obvious example would be a buggy whip maker in the early 1900's, who had to find a new job when horse transportation was replaced by cars. A new invention can radically change our lifestyle, our job, and even our family dynamics.

Remember back when people went to work for a company and stayed there for 30 years or more? On average most people now work for an employer only four years, and will hold a dozen different jobs in their lifetime[1].

Remember when most women stayed home and didn't work outside the home? In 1967, 49 percent of mothers stayed at home. That proportion steadily dropped through the decades until 1999, when only 23 percent of moms stayed

---

1. https://www.zippia.com/advice/average-nu mber-jobs-in-lifetime/

at home^2. The percentage is even smaller now. Whether a mom becomes a "stay at home" mom depends on a number of factors, including educational level and age. The higher the educational level the more likely that a woman will work outside the home. Some mothers with young children often opt to stay at home until they are sufficiently comfortable with their childcare situation, and are only then willing to return to working outside the home. Another change in family dynamics has been a rise in the number of "Mr. Moms," in which the one staying home with the children is the father rather the mother.

Did the evolutionary process enable us to cope well with change? I don't think so. The rapid pace of change has only been with us for a couple hundred years, and it is unlikely that the evolu-

---

2. https://www.bls.gov/opub/mlr/2014/beyond-bls/stay-at-home-mothers-through-the-years.htm

tionary process can work that quickly in humans. What are the main symptoms of failing to cope adequately with constant change in our lives? Anxiety is probably the most common symptom. According to psychologist Samanta Stein: "...the not-knowing is what causes anxiety. Even if we are excited about the change, since the results are unknowable and never fully in our control (because the future is never something we have full control over), we are anxious when thinking about it." So change causes anxiety and stress, even if the change is for the better. There are a number of other factors that can make change less anxiety-producing and more likely to give you new opportunities.

a. <u>Continuously and diligently monitor your life for change so it doesn't completely surprise you</u>.

Change is a lot more stressful when it takes you by surprise. One of the reasons why the recent Covid pandemic was so stressful and so deadly was because we didn't seem to see it coming and didn't adequately plan for it or respond quickly enough to it. You have to keep your head "on a swivel," because a change that can greatly affect your life can come from any direction. Meeting change head-on is particularly critical in business. History is replete with businesses that failed because they didn't change with the times...remember "Blockbuster." Pre-emptive change can help save a company. Being vigilant for change and rapidly adapting to it can be critical in the life of a company. As famous businessman Jack Welch once said: *Change before you have to.*

Change can demand anxiety-producing career changes. For example, it is probably only a matter of time until large trucks will be driven by computer software rather than drivers. Will this cause the loss of hundreds of thousands of truck driver jobs? If I were a truck driver, I would already be preparing for a career change.

b. <u>View change as an opportunity rather than as a stress.</u>

Socrates once said: "The secret of change is to focus all of your energy not on fighting the old, but on building the new." One of the exercises that businesses often do to keep up to date with change and their competition by doing a "SWOT" analysis. The goal of this exercise is to carefully analyze "Strengths, Weaknesses, Opportunities, and Threats." Such an analysis is frequently the first step in the process of developing a new business plan. It is clear that when change happens, there will be likely be "winners and losers." The losers will be those who failed to anticipate and adapt to the change and suffered considerable damage to their business and/or their personal circumstances. We need to do our own personal SWOT analysis, especially the part about opportunities. We should avoid the temptation to be a "one trick pony," in which we only know how to do one thing. Always take the opportunity to get training in other skills. This can be very helpful if your job is suddenly wiped out, because you might be able use your other skills to change gears and move on to an even more lucrative job.

In any field of medicine, change is particularly likely to occur suddenly and be disruptive. One example was the advent of antibiotics, which greatly challenged the field commonly referred to as Ear, Nose and Throat (ENT). (This is not their official name, but it is one most people can remember). Before antibiotics, people who got ear infections often went on to develop an abscess in the mastoid bone. This required surgical removal of the much or all of the mastoid bone (known as a mastoidectomy). When antibiotics were invented ear infections could be cured before they went on to develop mastoiditis. Suddenly one of the most common surgeries done by ENT doctors was largely eliminated. These doctors scrambled and subsequently developed a large number of very useful operations that not only helped humanity, but also assured their field's survival.

Another example occurred in my field, Physical Medicine & Rehabilitation. In the early days of our field many of our practitioners sub-specialized into the care and rehabilitation of those with polio. When the polio vaccines were invented, the incidence of new polio cases rather quickly went to zero in this country. I had a physician friend who was an expert in polio rehabilitation, and polio patients from around the country came to see him. Suddenly his polio practice was wiped out, and he had to start over doing rehabilitation of other serious problems such as brain injury and spinal cord injury. Although he quickly adapted and was able to continue his practice, he remained bitter about the loss of his polio practice. I was able to interview him near the end of his life and he was still bitter about losing his polio practice, even though the elimination of polio in this country was undeniably for the common good. Change frequently requires an "attitude adjustment." As Maya Angelou once said: "If you don't like something, change it. If you can't change it, change your attitude."

Keep in mind that when change occurs, the new reality causes opportunities to emerge that can be taken advantage of by those who anticipate them, quickly adapt to them, and ultimately profit from them.

c. <u>Lower your anxiety level by discussing changes that concern you with your family, friends and colleagues.</u>

I believe the worst way to handle stress is to "keep it bottled up" inside you. Any kind of stress, whether it is due to a death in the family or a loss of job, you can "let it out" by discussing it with others. Change is inevitable and being able to discuss it and its accompanying stress with friends and family and colleagues is an important psychological safety net. It is helpful "talk therapy," even if it doesn't come from a mental health professional.

When you talk with those similarly affected, you can immediately get a feeling that the stress of change is not only affecting you, but others as well. It can be very comforting to know that "you are not alone."

Another advantage of discussing the change with others who are similarly affected by it, is that you can listen to their ideas about how to "fix" the situation. Whether it is just a few people discussing the stress of change, or a large support group, listen to their ideas on how to fix it. One of them might come with an idea that hadn't even crossed your mind, but which is a brilliant and practical way of coping with the change situation.

Another advantage of talking out the change stress with friends and colleagues is it is a form of networking. This can be a major advantage for you from a job standpoint. One of them might give you a job or know of a job opportunity that would likely eliminate much of your job and financial stress.

The more of a crisis of change you find yourself in, the more you need family and friends to help you and support you. As Helen Keller once said: "Walking with a friend in the dark is better than walking alone in the light."

d. <u>Be willing to change</u>.

You have to be "rigidly flexible." Adaptability is essential for modern life, and it requires a willingness to change to meet the challenge of change. As Winston Churchill once said: "To improve is to change, to be perfect is to change often."

We have all met friends and family members who have a rigid personality and have difficulty with any kind of change, whether for the good or the bad. It is difficult to understand why they are this way, and my best explanation is that they are just "wired that way." My personal feeling is that this tendency to rigidity gets worse with age. You have heard the saying "set in their ways" to describe an elderly person who seems incapable of change. Some diseases increase this inflexibility.

For example, one of the changes that can occur early in a patient with Alzheimer's is that they have less tolerance for change. Even a relatively minor change in their lifestyle or daily routine can cause a marked emotional reaction. I am not an expert on how to deal with a rigid personality, but I suspect that these individuals have even more anxiety when change occurs than the rest of us. They especially require the help and support of friends and family to cope with anxiety-producing change. Their increased anxiety most likely makes it more difficult to seize on any opportunities produced by the change they are experiencing.

All of us should strive to be adaptable. Someone once said: "Things change. The only thing constant is change. It's up to you to be adaptable." -Anonymous. As author Jen Sincero said: "If you are serious about changing your life, you'll find a way. If you're not, you will find an excuse."

www.ingramcontent.com/pod-product-compliance
Lightning Source LLC
Chambersburg PA
CBHW060014050426
42448CB00012B/2751